GET BY IN ENGLISH

3

Pre-intermediate

コミュニケーションのための実践英語 3

［準中級編］

Julyan Nutt
Michael Marshall
Yoko Kurahashi
Manabu Miyata

SANSHUSHA

Preface

Get By In English is a basic English conversation series aimed primarily at non-English majors. It has been produced largely with the needs of Japanese university students in mind, based on the writers' experience of what language is needed and what challenges Japanese university students face. The series is composed of four books: *Starter*, *Elementary*, *Pre-intermediate* and *Intermediate*.

Each textbook includes a variety of activities such as pair work, listening comprehension and grammar practice. Where necessary, time-saving explanations in Japanese have been given about the tasks they are required to do, and about some key language points to assist the students (and teachers). Another feature of the book is that students are encouraged, with the help of their teachers, to produce short speeches in English related to the topic of each particular unit.

Vocabulary has been chosen to reflect the needs of the students and comprehensive glossaries (English / Japanese and Japanese / English) are included in the text. In addition, there are optional interview test questions for teachers as a means of grading and monitoring students' progress. Over the 15-week course, students will build confidence in expressing themselves through conversations and speeches.

This book, *Pre-intermediate*, is suitable for those students who are good at manipulating present continuous form, comparison and other basic expressions, in addition to simple present, past and future tenses. They are expected to learn such items as past continuous form, present perfect, countable / uncountable nouns, and so on. As this is the third-level book, Japanese explanations are fewer than those given in *Starter* and *Elementary*. Also, students are required to write speeches with less help from their teachers.

本書の構成と特徴

本書は、Prefaceで述べましたように、『コミュニケーションのための実践英語』シリーズ４冊のうちの３冊目にあたる準中級編です。現在・過去・未来の基本３時制や現在進行形あるいは比較構文などに習熟した学習者を想定しています。この準中級編では、それらの用法や構文に加えて、過去進行形や現在完了形などの構文や加算名詞・不加算名詞の用法などを学ぶことになります。

本シリーズは、主として英語を専門としない学生を対象とした基礎的な英会話のテキストです。著者であるネイティブ・スピーカー２人が日本の大学生を教えてきた長

年の経験に基づき、大学生にとって必要とされるのはどのような英語か、また、どのような課題に直面しているかということを念頭において、編集されています。本書の構成を特徴とともに紹介すると、以下のようになります。

①英語の授業を受ける際に必要となる最小限の表現と活動について学ぶためのWarm-up Unitから始めます。

②それに続く各ユニットを［Part A］と［Part B］に分け、［Part A］で基本となる語彙や表現を学び、［Part B］でそれを実際に用いる言語活動を行って、最後にスピーチで締めくくる、という構成になっています。

③［Part A］では、語彙の学習、発音とイントネーションの練習、モデルの対話文を用いた会話練習、文法問題、ペアで行う書き取り、と順に5つの段階を経て、必要な英語力を身につけます。

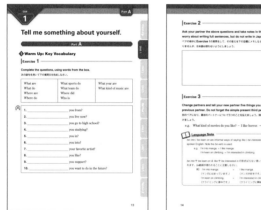
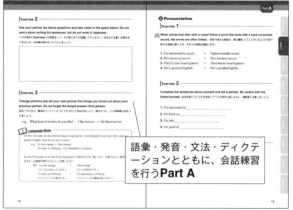

語彙・発音・文法・ディクテーションとともに、会話練習を行うPart A

④［Part B］では、リスニング問題に取り組みながら行う語彙の復習、ペアで行う会話練習、モデルとなるスピーチの学習、スピーチ原稿の作成、ペアの相手に行うスピーチ活動と、やはり順に5つの段階を経て、実践力を養います。

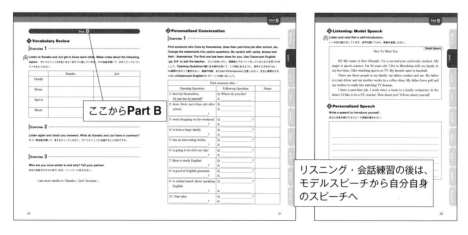

ここからPart B

リスニング・会話練習の後は、モデルスピーチから自分自身のスピーチへ

⑤３つのユニットを終えると、復習のためのReview Unitがあります。それまでの学習の成果を測るために、担当の先生が個人面接をする際にたずねる質問を想定した"Interview Test Questions"が最初に設けてありますので、先生の質問に答える準備をしてください。これに続く、適語選択問題、英文完成問題、並べ替え問題、質問文作成問題、読解問題は、クラスメートが面接を受けている間に各自で取り組むことになります。

⑥最初のReview Unit 1が終わると、同じように３つのユニットとReview Unit 2で学習します。こうして、Warm-up Unitに授業１回分（90分）、各ユニットに授業２回分（計12回分）、Review Unitに２回分という具合に、15回分の学習内容が１冊に収めてあります。

⑦本書では、与えられたタスクの内容や文法に関する重要なポイントについて、日本語の説明が加えてありますが、準中級レベルの学習者を意識して、必要最小限に抑えてあります。

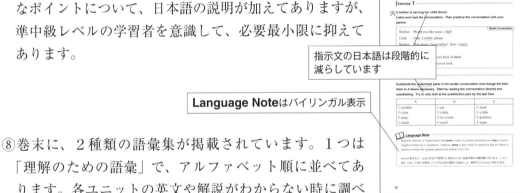

⑧巻末に、２種類の語彙集が掲載されています。１つは「理解のための語彙」で、アルファベット順に並べてあります。各ユニットの英文や解説がわからない時に調べてください。もう１つは「発話のための語彙」で、ペア活動の際に役立つ語彙を、トピック別にアイウエオ順にまとめました。日本語に相当する英語がわからない時に活用してください。

本書を用いた学習で、大学生として必要とされる英会話力がつくことを願っています。

著者一同

Table of Contents

Welcome to English Class!

◆1 Classroom English

In English class, try to speak English as much as possible. Here are some useful questions or expressions. 授業中にはできる限り英語で話すようにしなさい。よく使う表現を覚えましょう。

| Exercise 1

Read the following dialogues. Choose the correct sentences from the box.

次の会話の空所になっている箇所に次ページの一覧表から適する表現を選んで入れなさい。

1. Teacher: Now, can you turn to page 105?

Student : _____

Teacher: Sorry, ... Turn to... page ... one hundred... and... five.

Student : _____

Teacher: Sure, ... Page... one hundred... and... five.

2. Student : _____

Teacher: That's adjective.

Student : _____

Teacher: A, D, J, E, C, T, I, V, E.

3. Student : _____

Teacher: SYL – la – ble.

Student : Thank you.

4. Student : _____

Teacher: It means an extra question.

Student : Oh, I see. Thanks.

5. Student: _____

Teacher: Sure, go ahead.

Student: When is the end of term test?

Teacher: In two weeks. On January 25th.

6. Student: _____

Teacher: Yes, but please put it in your bag when you have finished.

Student: Okay, I will.

7. Student: _____

Teacher: Yes. How can I help?

Student: _____

Teacher: Of course, I'll play it again.

May I ask a question?	Can we listen to that again?
May I use my *smartphone dictionary*?	Please say that again.
How do you pronounce this word?	Please speak more slowly.
How do you say 形容詞 in English?	Excuse me! (*To call the teacher, you*
How do you spell *adjective* (*that*)?	*can raise your hand and say, 'Excuse*
What does *follow-up question* (*this word*) mean?	*me!'*)

Exercise 2

Practice the conversations with your partner. One of you plays the role of teacher, the other the student. Now change roles. ペアの相手と教師役・学生役を交替しながら、**Exercise 1**で完成した会話を練習しなさい。

Language Note

In English, it is usually natural to use the teacher's name like "Mr. Smith" or "Ms. Hayashi," not say "Teacher." Use the name the teacher asks you to use.

英語で先生に話しかける時には、"Teacher"とは言いません。"Mr. Smith"とか"Ms. Hayashi"のように、先生の名前を言うのが普通です。先生が指示する言い方で呼びかけるようにしなさい。

 Practice patterns

1) **Read the practice explanations in both English and Japanese. Choose the practice pattern from the box and write it in the correct place.** 英語と日本語の練習の説明を読んで、選択肢から練習の型を選び、適した場所に記入しなさい。

Practice Patterns

The followings are typical Practice Patterns in this class.

Five-finger Challenge	Changing Partners
Read, Remember, Repeat	Key Point Shadowing

---

1. _____

Students practice a dialog, but do not read the dialog directly. Each line they read to themselves, and remember it. Then repeat without looking. The aim is to learn (memorize) the dialog pattern.

会話文を読まないで、会話の練習をしなさい。まず、黙読して覚えなさい。つぎに、見ないで会話文を繰り返しなさい。この練習の目的は会話のパターンを学ぶことです。

2. _____

Students have a conversation. Each time they speak, they count one finger. Once both students have counted five times, the challenge is complete.

英語で会話をします。会話をするたびに、指を使って数えなさい。2人が5回ずつ数えたら、練習は終了です。(5回の取り組み)

3. _____

One student listens carefully to the other. They then try to repeat the key point that they hear.

相手の言うことをよく聞きます。つぎに聞こえたキーポイントを繰り返します。

4. _____

After each exercise, half of the class should move seats and find a new partner. The next week, the other half of the class will move.

練習が終わるたびに、クラスの半数が席を移動して新しいペアの相手と組みます。翌週は他の半数が移動します。

❸ Nice to meet you!

Exercise 1

Complete the answers with information about yourself.

まず、次の質問に答えて"**Myself**"の欄に記入しなさい。

	Myself	My partner
Where are you from?	I'm from _____	_____
Where do you live?	I live in _____	_____
What do you do?	I'm a _____	_____
What's your major?	My major is _____	_____
What do you do in your free time?	I like to _____ in my free time.	_____
Do you have a part-time job?	Yes, _____ No, I don't.	_____
How many hours a week do you work?	I work _____ hours a week.	_____
When's your birthday?	My birthday is on _____	_____
How do you come to college?	I come to college by _____	_____
How long does it take you to come to college?	It takes about _____	_____

Exercise 2

Now ask your partner the questions.

つぎにペアの相手に質問し、その答えを"**My partner**"の欄に記入しなさい。

Exercise 3

Change partners and take turns asking your new partner the questions.

別のペアになり、新しいパートナーと質問し合いなさい。

Exercise 4

Tell your new partner about your previous partner.

新しいパートナーに前のパートナーから聞いたことを伝えなさい。

📖 Language Note

When you are asked a "Do you.....?" question, it is grammatically correct to just answer "Yes" (Yes, I do) or "No" (No, I don't). However, in real conversations, it is more common (and polite!) to answer by giving a little more information.

    e.g. A: "Do you have a part-time job?"
          B: "Yes. I work in a supermarket."

"Do you.....?" とたずねられた時、単に "Yes"（Yes, I do）とか "No"（No, I don't）とだけ答えても、間違いではありません。しかし、実際の会話では、上の例にあるように、もう少し情報を添えるのが普通で、丁寧な答え方になります。

"What do you do?" does not mean "What are you doing?" In English, asking *What do you do?* is more natural than asking *What is your job?*

"What do you do?" は「今、何をしていますか？」という意味ではありません。相手の職業を聞く場合、What do you do? は What is your job? よりも自然な表現なのです。

4 Note on speeches

From Unit 1 you will prepare and make short speeches in English. The textbook will give you advice and hints about what to write. Ask your teacher for help if you need it.（Don't be shy!）You will read your speech to your conversation partner. You will also listen to other students' speeches. Writing and reading speeches aloud will help you practice your English more. Good luck!

スピーチについて

次のユニットから、英語で短いスピーチをすることになります。スピーチについてのヒントや助言はテキストにありますが、必要に応じて先生にたずねてください。恥ずかしがらずに聞くことです。準備ができたら、パートナー相手にスピーチしたり、逆に相手のスピーチを聞いたりします。スピーチ原稿を書いたり、読んだりすることは、とても良い練習になります。成功を祈ります！

> Enjoy your class!
> 授業を楽しみましょう！

Tell me something about yourself.

❶ Warm Up: Key Vocabulary

Exercise **1**

Complete the questions, using words from the box.

次の語句を用いて下の質問文を完成しなさい。

What are	What sports do	What year are
What do	What team do	What kind of music are
Where are	Where did	
Where do	Who is	

1. _____ you from?

2. _____ you live now?

3. _____ you go to high school?

4. _____ you studying?

5. _____ you in?

6. _____ you into?

7. _____ your favorite artist?

8. _____ you like?

9. _____ you support?

10. _____ you want to do in the future?

Exercise 2

Ask your partner the above questions and take notes in the space below. Do not worry about writing full sentences, but do not write in Japanese.

ペアの相手に**Exercise 1**の質問をして、その答えを下の空欄にメモしなさい。完全な文を書く必要はありませんが、日本語は使わないようにしましょう。

Exercise 3

Change partners and tell your new partner five things you found out about your previous partner. Do not forget the simple present third person.

別のペアになり、最初のパートナーについて5つのことを伝えましょう。例のように、三人称単数に気をつけましょう。

    e.g.   What kind of movies do you like? – I like horror. → He likes horror.

 Language Note

be into / *be keen on* are informal ways of saying *like* / *be interested in* and are often used in spoken English. Note the *be* verb is used.

       e.g.   I'm into manga. = I like manga.

            I'm keen on climbing. = I'm interested in climbing.

be into や *be keen on* は *like* や *be interested in* の形式ばらない言い方で、口語ではよく使用されます。*be*動詞が使われることに注意しなさい。

例）I'm into manga.	=	I like manga.
（マンガにはまっています。）		（マンガが好きです。）
I'm keen on climbing.	=	I'm interested in climbing.
（クライミングに夢中です。）		（クライミングに興味があります。）

❷ Pronunciation

Exercise 1

When words that start with a vowel follow a word that ends with a hard consonant sound, the words are often linked. 母音で始まる単語が、硬口蓋音（こうこうがいおん）の子音で終わる単語に続くとき、それらの単語は連結します。

1. I'm interested in music.   →   I'**m**intereste**d**in music.

2. He's keen on soccer.   →   He's kee**n**on soccer.

3. They're into board games.   →   They'**re**into board games.

4. She's good at English.   →   She's goo**d**a**t**English.

Exercise 2

Complete the sentences about yourself and tell a partner. Be careful with the linked sounds. 自分自身について文を完成してペアの相手に話しなさい。連結音に注意しましょう。

1. I'm interested in _____.

2. I'm keen on _____.

3. I'm into _____.

4. I'm good at _____.

Exercise 3

Change partners and tell your new partner what you found out about your previous partner.

❸ Model Conversation

Exercise 1

05 **Sanae and Yusuke are getting to know each other.** 初対面のサナエとユウスケが話しています。

Listen and read the conversation. Then practice the conversation with your partner. 2人の会話を聞いてから、音読しなさい。その後、ペアになって、この会話を練習しなさい。

Model Conversation

Sanae　：　Tell me something about yourself.

Yusuke:　Well, I'm ①into ②rock music. I play ③the guitar.

Sanae　：　Wow, I didn't know that.

Yusuke:　How about you? What are you ①into?

Sanae: :　I really like to ④watch movies at home.

Exercise 2

Substitute the underlined parts in the model conversation. Start by reading the conversation directly and substituting. Try to only look at the substitution part by the last time. 上の会話の下線部(①〜④)を次の語句に入れ替えて、練習しなさい。 最後には会話文を見なくても言えるようにしましょう。

A	B	C
① good at	① interested in	① keen on
② sports	② board games	② video games
③ golf and tennis	③ every day after school	③ with people from other countries
④ practice *kendo*	④ draw my favorite characters	④ study languages

4 Grammar Exercises

Exercise 1

The following sentences are incorrect. (They are common mistakes of English learners in Japan!) Write a correct version of each sentence. (There maybe more than one correct way to rewrite the sentence.) 次の文は間違っています。(日本の英語学習者がよくする間違いです。)それぞれを正しい文に書き換えましょう。(正しい文が1つとは限りません。)

1. What do you like sports?

_____ .

2. My family is four people.

_____ .

3. Do your father like baseball?

_____ .

4. My sister have long hair.

_____ .

5. Where country are you from?

_____ .

6. My brother don't have a part-time job.

_____ .

7. I like to go to shopping.

_____ .

8. Next weekend we go to the beach.

_____ .

9. I like food is sushi.

_____ .

10. Last night I stay home and watch TV.

_____ .

Unscramble the words to make a correct reply. Then match the replies to the questions next page.　単語を並べ替えて正しい文を作り、Bに書き入れなさい。つぎに、Bのような答えとなる質問文を次ページから選びなさい。

1. A: _____ ?

  B: _____ .
   [born / Osaka / I / was / in]

2. A: _____ ?

  B: _____ .
   [the piano / yes / can / play / I]

3. A: _____ ?

  B: _____ .
   [student / I'm / a]

4. A: _____ ?

  B: _____ .
   [prefer / soccer / but / I / yes]

5. A: _____ ?

  B: _____ .
   [father / three / mother / my / me / and]

6. A: _____ ?

  B: _____ .
   [Niigata / in / live / I]

7. A: _____ ?

  B: _____ .
   [was / in / I / born / 2001]

8. A: _____ ?

  B: _____ .
   [a bookstore / I / in / yes / work]

9. A: _____?

B: _____.

[bus / by / here / I / come]

10 A: _____?

B: _____.

[Korean / she's / in / interested / dramas]

---

a) When were you born?

b) How do you come to school?

c) Can you play a musical instrument?

d) What do you do?

e) Where do you live?

f) What does your mother like?

g) Where were you born?

h) Do you like rugby?

i) How many people are there in your family?

j) Do you have a part-time job?

---

⑤ Pair Dictation

Student A: Turn to page 95.

Aさん：95ページを見なさい。

Student B: Turn to page 103.

Bさん：103ページを見なさい。

❶ Vocabulary Review

Exercise 1

Listen to Kanako and Juri get to know each other. Make notes about the following topics. カナコとジュリがお互いをよく知ろうと話しています。その会話を聞いて、次のトピックについてメモをとりなさい。

	Kanako	Juri
Family		
Home		
Sports		
Music		

Exercise 2

Listen again and check your answers. What do Kanako and Juri have in common?
もう一度会話を聞いて、答えをチェックしなさい。カナコとジュリに共通することは何ですか。

Exercise 3

Who are you more similar to and why? Tell your partner.
あなた自身がどちらに似ているか、パートナーに伝えなさい。

I am more similar to (Kanako / Juri) because....

❷ Personalized Conversation

Exercise 1

Find someone who lives by themselves, does their part-time job after school, etc. Change the statements into yes/no questions. Be careful with *verbs*, *tenses* and *their / themselves*. The first one has been done for you. Use Classroom English (pp. 8-9) to ask the teacher. ひとり住まいの人、授業後にアルバイトをしている人などを見つけましょう。**Opening Question**の欄にある語句を用いて、1)の例にあるように、相手にたずねるYes / No疑問文を作って書きなさい。動詞や時制、また*their*や*themselves*に注意しなさい。先生に質問をするときには**Classroom English**（8〜9ページ）を使いましょう。

Find someone who…		
Opening Question	Follow-up Question	Name
1) lives by themselves. *Do you live by yourself?*	Q: Where do you live? A: _____	
2) does their part-time job after school. _____ ?	Q: _____ A: _____	
3) went shopping on the weekend. _____ ?	Q: _____ ? A: _____	
4) is from a large family. _____ ?	Q: _____ ? A: _____	
5) has an interesting hobby. _____ ?	Q: _____ ? A: _____	
6) is going to be rich one day! _____ ?	Q: _____ ? A: _____	
7) likes to study English. _____ ?	Q: _____ ? A: _____	
8) is good at English grammar. _____ ?	Q: _____ ? A: _____	
9) is embarrassed about speaking English. _____ ?	Q: _____ ? A: _____	
10) *Your idea* _____ ?	Q: _____ ? A: _____	

Exercise 2

Think of a follow-up question for the second column. It should be a *Wh question*.
Follow-up Questionの欄に、最初の質問に続くWH疑問文を考えて書きなさい。

Exercise 3

Get to know your classmates by asking these questions.
次のルールに従って、クラスメートのことを知る活動をしましょう。

Rules: You can only write a student who answers, "yes" to the first question.

You can only write a student's name once.

You must form a pair and ask each other, not in a group.

You should only use English.

ルール：最初の質問に「はい」と答えた学生の名前をNameの欄に書くことができま
す。

1人の学生の名前は1回だけNameの欄に書くことができます。

グループではなく、ペアを組んで質問し合いなさい。

英語のみを使用しなさい。

❸ Listening: Model Speech

Listen and read Ren's self-introduction.

レンが自己紹介をしています。音声を聞いてから、原稿を音読しなさい。

Model Speech

Nice To Meet You

Hi! My name is Ren Okazaki. I'm a second-year university student. My major is sports science. I'm 20 years old. I live in Hiroshima with my family. In my free time, I like watching sports on TV. My favorite sport is baseball.

There are three people in my family: my father, mother and me. My father is a taxi driver and my mother works in a coffee shop. My father loves golf and my mother is really into watching TV dramas.

I have a part-time job. I work twice a week in a family restaurant. In the future I'd like to be a P.E. teacher. How about you? Tell me about yourself!

---

❹ Personalized Speech

Write a speech to introduce yourself.

あなた自身を紹介するスピーチ原稿を書きなさい。

5 Speech: Pair Discussion

Exercise 1

Now work in pairs. Read your speech to your conversation partner. Listen carefully to your partner's speech. ペアになってスピーチ原稿を読み、相手に聞いてもらいなさい。交替して、相手のスピーチをしっかり聞いてあげましょう。

Exercise 2

Ask your partner questions. First, write 3 follow-up questions. 例にならって、ペアの相手にたずねる質問を3つ書きなさい。すでにスピーチで聞いたことを質問しないように注意しましょう。

Examples of questions:

What kind of _____ do you like?

Can you _____ ?

Tell me (more) about your _____ .

MY QUESTIONS

1. _____ ?

2. _____ ?

3. _____ ?

Exercise 3

Now ask your questions.

Exercise 4

Take two minutes to memorize your speech. Then, close the textbook and try to make the speech again. (It is not important to repeat your speech perfectly, just try to remember as much as you can!)

2分でスピーチを覚えなさい。覚えたら、テキストを閉じてもう一度スピーチをしなさい。(完璧なスピーチでなくてもかまいません。できる限り見ないで言えるようにしましょう。)

Unit 2

Could you hand in your homework by Friday?

Part A

1 Warm Up: Key Vocabulary

Exercise 1

Match the duties and chores to the picture. 義務や必要な仕事が一覧表になっています。それ

ぞれの表現に合う絵を答えなさい。

Duties		Chores	
1. (　) finish the report	☐	6. (　) clean your room	☐
2. (　) give a presentation	☐	7. (　) take out the trash	☐
3. (　) hand in your homework	☐	8. (　) drop off the dry cleaning	☐
4. (　) speak to your tutor	☐	9. (　) check the mailbox	☐
5. (　) prepare for the exam	☐	10. (　) wash the dishes	☐

a.

b.

c.

d.

e.

f.

Exercise 2

Which of these duties or chores do you have to do? Check ☑ them in the box.

あなたは、これらの義務と必要な仕事のどれをしなくてはいけませんか。前ページの□に✓を記入しなさい。

Exercise 3

Do you have any deadlines? By when do you have to do them? Write them down and tell a partner. 締め切りはありますか。いつしなくてはいけませんか。下に書き出して、ペアの相手に伝えなさい。

e.g. I have to hand in my homework by next week.

I have to take out the trash on Saturdays and Wednesdays.

1. _____

2. _____

3. _____

4. _____

📖 Language Note

The words *by* and *until* are often confused: *by* means something **happens** *by* a certain time; *until* means something **continues** *until* a certain time.

by と *until* はよく混同されます。byは何かがある時までに起こることを意味します。*until*はある時まで何かが続くことを意味します。

❷ Pronunciation

The soft "v" in *have to* is often pronounced with a harder "f" sound i.e. *haft'*. Also, has to is pronounced *hast'*. The long "to" sound is shortened to "t'." Listen to the examples.

*have to*のv のやわらかい音は*haft'*のように強めのfでよく発音されます。また、has toは*hast'*と発音されます。toはt'と短くなります。例を聞きなさい。

e.g. I **haft**'hand in my homework by next week.

John **hast**'clean his room by the weekend.

Tell a new partner about your duties and chores, and those of your previous partner. Be careful with the pronunciation of *haft'* and *hast'*.

📖 Language Note

Many native speakers often use *have/has got to* instead of *have/has to*. When they speak quickly this often sounds like *gotta*. (Example: It's late. I ('ve) gotta go!) *gotta* is not standard written English, though some people use it in casual online messages, etc.

*have/has to*の代わりに*have/has got to*を使うネイティブスピーカーがたくさんいます。早口で話すと、例えば、*It's late. I ('ve) gotta go!* のように *gotta*と聞こえることがよくあります。*gotta*は標準的な書き言葉ではありませんが、オンラインでのくだけた通信文などで使う人もいます。

❸ Model Conversation

Exercise 1

Jane is talking with Mrs. Roberts about her homework.
Listen and read the conversation. Then practice the conversation with your partner.

	Model Conversation
Mrs. Roberts :	Could you ①hand in your homework by ②Friday?
Jane :	By ②Friday? Sorry, I won't have time. I have to ③study all day today. Then I'm ④preparing for an exam tomorrow.
Mrs. Roberts :	How about by ⑤Monday, then?
Jane :	⑤Monday? That will be fine.

Exercise 2

Substitute the underlined parts in the model. Start by reading the conversation directly and substituting. Try to only look at the substitution part by the last time.

A	B	C
① tidy your room	① finish the report	① drop off the dry cleaning
② Sunday	② the 21st	② 10:00 a.m.
③ practice baseball on Saturday morning	③ go on a business trip on the 19th	③ practice soccer from 7:00 a.m.
④ meeting my friend in the afternoon	④ visiting customers on the 20th	④ having lunch with John
⑤ Tuesday	⑤ the 25th	⑤ 5:00 p.m.

 **Language Note**

The present continuous is often used when discussing events in the near future.

現在進行形は近い将来の出来事を話す時によく使用されます。

28

④ Grammar Exercises

Exercise **1**

A) Complete the sentences with the phrases below. (The phrases may be used more than once.)

| have to | don't have to | has to | doesn't have to |

1. In Japan most high school students _____ wear a uniform.

2. Tomorrow is a holiday. I _____ go to school.

3. My friend is in the basketball club. He _____ practice hard every day.

4. He is rich! He _____ work at all!

5. The entrance ticket is ¥500. However, it is free for elementary school students. They _____ pay anything.

6. My mother works in a department store. She usually _____ work on Saturdays and Sundays.

7. My friend lives very near the college. He can walk here. He _____ take the train.

8. I want to study abroad next year, so I _____ save a lot of money.

B) Write *true* sentences about you and your family member.

1. Every morning I have to _____.

2. Next weekend I have to _____, but I don't have to _____.

3. My (_____) has to _____, but doesn't have to _____.

Exercise 2

Before you start: Can you say the months in English? Say them by yourself or to your partner.

あなたは、英語で12か月の名前を言えますか？　1人で、あるいはペアの相手に言ってみましょう。

Write today's date: _____.
今日の日付を書きなさい。

Now write the correct dates below. (The usual order is *month then number*. Note the way numbers are written. Example: Christmas Day – December 25th.)

下にあげた特定の日の日付を書きなさい。（通常、まず月の名前、つぎに数字が続きます。数字の書き方に注意しなさい。例えば、クリスマスはDecember 25thとなります。）

New Year's Day _____

Valentine's Day _____

Halloween _____

Christmas Eve _____

New Year's Eve _____

My birthday _____

(　　　　　)'s birthday _____

The next English class _____

⑤ Pair Dictation

Student A: Turn to page 96.　　　　**Student B: Turn to page 104.**

Part B

1 Vocabulary Review

Exercise 1

🎧 **Listen to the conversation. Adam is talking to his boss. What does she ask him to do and by when does he agree to do it? Write his duty and agreed deadline in the appropriate place in the diary below.**

アダムが上司と話している会話を聞いて、彼のすべきこととその締め切り（曜日と時間）がいつになったかを下の表に書き入れなさい。

	Morning	Afternoon
Monday, May 20th		
Tuesday, May 21st		
Wednesday, May 22nd		
Thursday, May 23rd		
Friday, May 24th		
Saturday, May 25th		

Exercise 2

Now listen again and fill in the Adam's busy schedule.

Personalized Conversation

Exercise 1

Complete the diary on the left with your plans, commitments and deadlines for next week.

My diary	a.m.	p.m.
Sun.		
Mon.		
Tue.		
Wed.		
Thu.		
Fri.		
Sat.		

My partner's diary	a.m.	p.m.
Sun.		
Mon.		
Tue.		
Wed.		
Thu.		
Fri.		
Sat.		

Exercise 2

Change partners and tell each other about your schedules. Do not look at each other's diary, but use Key Point Shadowing and classroom English to communicate.

e.g. A: I am doing my part-time job all day on Sunday.

B: All day on Sunday?

A: Yes, that's right. Then on Monday I have an English class in the morning.

B: Did you say "English class"?

A: Yes, I did. On Monday morning.

B: OK. I got it.

❸ Listening: Model Speech

 Listen and read Ayame's speech about her part-time job.

> ⌐ Model Speech ⌐
>
> ### My Part-Time Job
>
> My part-time job is in a Japanese restaurant, which is called *izakaya* in Japanese. I work there three times a week: on Thursdays, Fridays and Saturdays. I usually work from 6:00 p.m. to 11:00 p.m., but sometimes I work overtime.
>
> In my job I have to take orders from customers, serve them food and drinks and sometimes work at the cash register. I usually enjoy my job. My boss is kind and my co-workers are very friendly. Also, I can meet and talk to many interesting customers. I don't have to cook food in the kitchen, so my job is quite easy. The hourly pay is good and it is also near my house.
>
> However, sometimes we are very busy and I get very tired, especially on Friday evenings. Also, if I make a mistake or serve the customers late, they can become angry!
>
> Many students find their part-time job on the Internet, but I was introduced to this job by a friend. I will probably work there until I graduate from university.

◆4 Personalized Speech

Write a speech about your part-time job. (If you don't have a part-time job, you can write about your previous job, *using the past tense.* If you have never worked, write about a job you would like to do.) あなたのアルバイトについてスピーチ原稿を書きなさい。（もし、アルバイトをしていないなら、過去形を用いて、以前していたアルバイトについて書いてもかまいません。もし、アルバイトをしたことがないなら、やってみたいアルバイトについて書きなさい。）

_____

_____

_____

_____

_____

_____

_____

_____

_____

_____

◆5 Speech: Pair Discussion

| Exercise 1 ─────────────────────

Now work in pairs. Read your speech to your conversation partner. Listen carefully to your partner's speech.

Exercise 2

Ask your partner questions. First, write 3 follow-up questions.
Note: if your partner doesn't have a part-time job, look at the B) examples of questions.

A) Examples of questions to students who *have* part-time jobs:

How did you find your job?

What do you like most about your job?

Do you have to _____?

B) Examples of questions to students who *don't have* part-time jobs:

Are you looking for a part-time job now?

Would you like to work in a _____?

Are you going to get a job this year?

MY QUESTIONS

1. _____?

2. _____?

3. _____?

Exercise 3

Now ask your questions.

Exercise 4

Take two minutes to memorize your speech. Then, close the textbook and try to make the speech again. (It is not important to repeat your speech perfectly, just try to remember as much as you can!)

3

Where were you when the earthquake happened?

Part A

1 Warm Up: Key Vocabulary

Exercise 1

Look at the four pictures about disasters. Label the pictures with phrases from the box.

An earthquake happened.	An accident happened.
A typhoon hit.	A volcano erupted.

1.

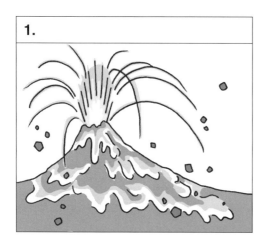

2.

3.

4.

Exercise 2

Choose words from the box to complete the news reports. (Some words are used more than once.)

(14)

accident	earthquake	typhoon	volcano
erupted	hit	damaged	injured

a) Yesterday at 2:45 p.m. there was a serious _____ on Route 66. A man was driving too fast when he hit another car. Nobody was _____ .

b) At 6:15 a.m. on Sunday morning, there was a strong _____ in northern Hokkaido. Most people were still sleeping, but no houses were _____ .

c) At 10:05 a.m. on Saturday morning, a _____ _____ in New Zealand. A group of people were hiking on the mountain. Two people were _____ and taken to a hospital.

d) The _____ _____ the Tokai area at 7:15 a.m. on Monday morning. Some buildings were _____ and schools were closed in the morning.

Exercise 3

Practice reading the news reports to your partner. Read one sentence at a time. Use "Read, Remember, Repeat."

❷ Pronunciation

| Exercise 1

 **Often native speakers do not clearly pronounce the *ng* sound at the end of a word, especially in casual conversation.**

ネイティブスピーカーは単語の最後にくる*ng*の音をはっきりと発音しないことが、特に日常会話で多くなります。

e.g.   What were you doing?   I was watching a movie.
         What were you doin'?   I was watchin' a movie.

Listen to the reduced forms of the past continuous in the following sentences.

1. What were you doin' this morning?   I was playin' golf.
2. Where were you sittin' yesterday?   I was sittin' next to John.
3. Where were they yesterday?   They were at home, watchin' TV.
4. Were you cookin' here this afternoon?   No, I wasn't.
5. Why were you walkin' so fast?   I was late for class.

| Exercise 2

Practice asking and answering the questions and answers with your partner. Remember, people drop the *g* sound in *ing* because it is easier to say. It sounds strange if you pause in the sentence. Try "Read, Remember, Repeat." Think about pronunciation, stress and intonation, then say.

❸ Model Conversation

Exercise 1

Maki and Saki are talking about their band practice.
Listen and read the conversation. Then practice the conversation with your partner.

> Model Conversation
>
> Maki: Where were you ①at seven this morning?
>
> Saki : I was ② at home
>
> Maki: ③We had band practice.
>
> Saki : Sorry, I was ④ sleeping.

Exercise 2

Substitute the underlined parts in the model conversation. Start by reading the conversation directly and substituting. Try to only look at the substitution part by the last time.

A	B	C
① when the earthquake happened ② doing my part-time job ③ I was worried about you ④ going to call	① on Friday night ② in my office ③ We had a date ④ working late	① when you heard the news ② listening to the radio in my car ③ I tried to call you ④ driving

4 Grammar Exercises

Exercise 1

Circle the correct form of the verb in the following sentences.

1. This morning I *got up/was getting up, ate/was eating* breakfast and *went/was going* to school.

2. She *watched/was watching* TV when her mobile phone *rang/was ringing.*

3. It *rained/was raining* when they got up yesterday, so they *didn't go out/weren't going out.*

4. I'm very hungry. I *didn't eat/wasn't eating* lunch today.

5. When the accident *happened/was happening,* I *walked/was walking* to the station.

6. Last year Kenji *went/was going* abroad for the first time.

7. Sorry, I *didn't hear/wasn't hearing* you. I *didn't listen/wasn't listening*!

8. What *did you do/were you doing* this time yesterday?

9. My soccer team *won/was winning* the last game.

10. My soccer team *lost/was losing* when I scored a goal in the last minute. We were so happy!

Exercise 2

Try to make *true* sentences about you and your family member.

1. When the teacher entered the classroom, many of the students were

_____.

2. I was _____ when _____.

3. This time yesterday I was _____.

4. I was _____ when my (   )

_____.

5 Pair Dictation

Student A: Turn to page 97.   Student B: Turn to page 105.

1 Vocabulary Review

Exercise 1

(17) Listen to the story about the earthquake. Where were Yuri's family when the earthquake happened and what were they doing? Complete the table with notes.

	During		After
	Where?	What?	What?
Yuri's father			
Yuri's mother			
Yuri			
Daisuke			

Exercise 2

Listen again. What did they do after the earthquake?

Exercise 3

In pairs practice telling the story to each other.

2 Personalized Conversation

Exercise 1&2

Student A: Witness
Turn to page 98.

Student B: Police Officer
Turn to page 106.

Work with your partner to write a police report. Remember to use the third person and be careful with tenses. パートナーと協力して捜査報告（警察の調書）を書きなさい。三人称を使用することを忘れないように、また時制に気をつけましょう。

Police Report

The witness is _____. He/She _____

_____

_____

_____

_____

_____

_____

_____

_____

_____

_____

_____

_____

_____

_____

_____

_____

_____

③ Listening: Model Speech

Listen and read about Shota's weekend.

(18)

(Model Speech)

My Weekend

My weekend was kind of fun. On Saturday I got up early: at about 7 o'clock, ate breakfast and took my dog for a walk. I had a lot of homework, so I studied for about three hours at home. After eating lunch, I took a nap. On Saturdays I have a part-time job in an Italian restaurant. I worked for five hours from 6:00 p.m. to 11:00 p.m. The restaurant was very busy last Saturday. There were so many customers. My co-workers and I were very tired. After work I went to eat *ramen* with two of my co-workers and we chatted until about 1:30 a.m., so I went to bed late.

On Sunday I got up late, maybe around 11:00 a.m. I didn't eat breakfast. I was relaxing at home when my friend Akira called me and invited me to go for lunch. We met at a restaurant, ate lunch and then went shopping. My friend bought a new pair of shoes. After that, we decided to go bowling. We bowled for about two hours. I got home at about 7:00 p.m. I have to get up early for school, so I usually go to bed early. Before going to bed, I watched a few music videos on YouTube.

④ Personalized Speech

Write a speech *in the past tense* about your weekend. (Don't worry if you think it wasn't so interesting!)

_____

_____

_____

_____

_____

_____

_____

_____

⑤ Speech: Pair Discussion

| Exercise 1

Now work in pairs. Read your speech to your conversation partner. Listen carefully to your partner's speech.

| Exercise 2

Ask your partner questions. First, write 3 follow-up questions.

> Examples of questions:
>
> Did you enjoy the weekend?
>
> Did you _____?
>
> What are you going to do next weekend?

MY QUESTIONS

1. _____?
2. _____?
3. _____?

| Exercise 3

Now ask your questions.

| Exercise 4

Take two minutes to memorize your speech. Then, close the textbook and try to make the speech again. (It is not important to repeat your speech perfectly, just try to remember as much as you can!)

1 Interview Test Questions

Answer the questions about yourself with complete sentences.

次の質問に主語・述語のある完全な英文で答えなさい。

 1. What are you interested in?

_____

2. What sports do you like?

_____

3. What kind of music are you into?

_____

4. Who is your favorite artist?

_____

5. What chores do you have to do?

_____

6. Are you having a busy week?

_____

7. Do you have any deadlines?

_____

8. What are you doing on the weekend?

_____

9. Where were you at 9:00 this morning?

_____

10. What were you doing?

_____

11. When did the Tohoku earthquake happen?

_____

12. Do you remember what you were doing then?

_____

Warm-up

Unit 1

Unit 2

Unit 3

Review 1

Unit 4

Unit 5

Unit 6

Review 2

 Grammar

Circle the correct word(s). 空所に入る語句を選んで、正しい英文を完成しなさい。

1. I _____up late yesterday.

[got / was getting / will get]

2. _____ a big typhoon last week.

[There is / There are / There was]

3. I _____ lunch when the earthquake happened.

[was eating / ate / will eat]

4. In this class we _____ study English.

[have to / has to / doesn't have to]

5. Before _____ to bed, I watched TV.

[go / going / went]

6. My sister _____ study for a test tomorrow.

[have to / has to / had to]

7. Where _____ you born?

[is / was / were]

8. It's free! You _____ pay anything.

[have to / don't have to / will]

❸ Vocabulary

Write the words below in the correct spaces. (Change the words to plural if necessary.)次の各文の空所に適した単語を選び、必要に応じて正しい形にして記入しなさい。

accident	customer	dish	dry cleaning	earthquake
hobby	language	month	trash	typhoon

1. My father's _____ is golf. He loves it!

2. How many _____ do you speak?

3. There was a big _____ in Tohoku in 2001.

4. I work in the kitchen. I have to wash the _____.

5. Japan has many _____ every year. It rains a lot and it is very windy.

6. February is the shortest _____ of the year.

7. My part-time job was very busy last night. There were many _____.

8. Please take out the _____ on Monday morning.

9. I'm going to take this suit to the _____ store.

10. There was a car _____ near my house but luckily nobody was injured.

Warm-up

Unit 1

Unit 2

Unit 3

Review 1

Unit 4

Unit 5

Unit 6

Review 2

◆ Writing I

Put the sentences in the correct order. (**There may be more than one correct order in some sentences.**)次の語群を並べ替えて、正しい英文を書きなさい。

1. sports / what / like / you / do

_____.

2. mother / is / into / my / badminton

_____.

3. room / by / could / tidy / you / your / tomorrow

_____?

4. have / study / to / you / hard

_____!

5. doing / morning / you / this / were / what

_____?

6. coming / is / a typhoon / tomorrow

_____.

7. tomorrow / you / have / work / to / do

_____?

8. third-year / she's / a / student / university

_____.

9. studying/ when / I / you / called / was

_____.

10. last / an earthquake / night / was / there

_____.

⑤ Writing II

Write a question that matches each answer. (There may be more than one correct question.) Bのような答えとなる質問文を考えて書きなさい。

1. A: _____ ?
   B: My father? He's a dentist.

2. A: _____ ?
   B: She's in the second year.

3. A: _____ ?
   B: My birthday? It's May 2nd.

4. A: _____ ?
   B: I'm really into playing video games.

5. A: _____ ?
   B: No, he lives with his family.

6. A: _____ ?
   B: Yes, I work in a bookstore.

7. A: _____ ?
   B: I usually have to work on Fridays and Saturdays.

8. A: _____ ?
   B: I was born in 2002.

9. A: _____ ?
   B: This morning? I was working.

10. A: _____ ?
   B: No, it's a holiday, so I don't have to go to school.

Warm-up

Unit 1

Unit 2

Unit 3

Review 1

Unit 4

Unit 5

Unit 6

Review 2

◆6 Comprehension

Read Gaku's blog post about Typhoon number 15. Answer the questions with complete sentences. ガクが書いた台風15号のブログ記事を読み、下の問いに主語・述語のある完全な文で答えなさい。

Thursday, September 23rd

Typhoon number 15 hit Ise at 4:00 this morning. Most people were sleeping when it hit, but I was working. I have a part-time job at an Internet cafe. I work at night because the pay is better. It was very windy and I was worried because I did not think I could go back home. Seven people were injured and there was a lot of damage to buildings and trees. All schools in Ise will be closed until Monday morning. This is good news for me because I had to hand in a report by Friday. Now I do not have to do it until next week. Now my family has to clean our yard and prepare for the next typhoon. It is coming later next week!

1. When did Typhoon number 15 hit?

_____

2. What were most people doing then?

_____

3. Where does Gaku work?

_____

4. Why does he work at night?

_____

5. How many people were injured?

_____

6. What was damaged?

_____

7. What happened to the schools?

_____

8. When will they open?

_____

9. Why is this good news for Gaku?

_____

10. When is his new deadline?

_____

11. What does his family have to do now?

_____

12. What is happening next week?

_____

_____

Warm-up

Unit 1

Unit 2

Unit 3

Review 1

Unit 4

Unit 5

Unit 6

Review 2

Have you ever been snowboarding?

Part A

1 Warm Up: Key Vocabulary

Exercise 1

Match the activities to the pictures.

go snowboarding	( )	meet a famous person	( )
ride in a helicopter	( )	speak a foreign language	( )
go white-water rafting	( )	eat unusual food	( )
try a bungee jump	( )	see a ghost	( )
spend a night in the hospital	( )	break a bone	( )
enter a marathon	( )	have an accident	( )
climb Mt. Fuji	( )	play mahjong	( )
visit a foreign country	( )	wrestle a sumo wrestler	( )

1.

2.

3.

4.

5.

6.

7.

8.

9.

10.

11.

12.

13.

14.

15.

16.

Exercise 2

Write the past participle next to the plain form.

be	_____	break	_____	have	_____
do	_____	try	_____	eat	_____
go	_____	meet	_____	catch	_____
ride	_____	speak	_____	lose	_____
fly	_____	see	_____	read	_____
take	_____	spend	_____	write	_____

📖 Language Note

To express experience 'have/has been' is often used (not have/has gone).

　　e.g. I have been skiing many times, but I've never been snowboarding.
　　　　Have you ever been abroad?

The word *gone* is used to show the person is still doing something.

　　e.g. He has *gone* to America. = He **went** to America and is **still there**.

The word *been* is used to show the person has finished the event.

　　e.g. He has *been* to America. = He **went** to America and **returned**.

経験を表すために'have/has been'がよく使用されます（have/has goneは使用しません）。

　　例）I have been skiing many times, but I've never been snowboarding.
　　　　（私は何回もスキーに行ったことがありますが、スノーボードはしたことがありません。）
　　　　Have you ever been abroad?
　　　　（海外に出かけたことがありますか？）

*gone*はまだ何かを行っていることを示すために使われます。

　　例）He has *gone* to America.　　　　=　　　　He **went** to America and is **still there**.
　　　　（彼はアメリカに行ってしまった。）　　　（彼はアメリカに行ってまだそこにいる。）

*been*は事柄が終了したことを示すために使われます。

　　例）He has *been* to America.　　　　=　　　　He **went** to America and **returned**.
　　　　（彼はアメリカに行ってきた。）　　　　（彼はアメリカに行って戻ってきた。）

Exercise 3

Complete the questions with the correct form of the verb(1~3) and add two ideas of your own(4&5).

1. Have you ever _____ (break) a bone?

2. Have you ever _____ (fly) in an airplane?

3. Have you ever _____ (meet) someone famous?

4. Have you ever _____ ?

5. Have you ever _____ ?

Exercise 4

Ask your partner five questions. Try to answer with extra information, not just *yes* or *no*.

> Example answers:
> Yes, I have. I did that four years ago.
> Yes, when I was five.
> No, I haven't, but I want to.
> No, but I'm going to try that soon.

Exercise 5

Change partners and tell your new partner two things you found out about your previous parter. Don't forget to include the extra information.

e.g.　Judy hasn't been snowboarding, but she wants to try.
　　　Maki has been to an interesting place. She visited Spain last summer.

 Pronunciation

Exercise 1

1) **Listen to the following questions and add stress marks (ˊ) to the stressed words.**

1. Have you ever been ice-skating?
2. Have you ever eaten something strange?
3. Have you ever visited a foreign country?
4. Have you ever tried a traditional Japanese craft?
5. Have you ever spent a night in the hospital?

2) **What types of words are stressed? Discuss with a partner.**

> **Language Note**
>
> Typically, the auxiliary verb in a Yes/No question (the first word) is not stressed. Many Japanese learners of English mistakenly believe it is.
>
> Yes/No疑問文の助動詞（最初の単語）には、大体は強勢が置かれません。日本人の英語学習者の多くは強勢が置かれると間違って考えています。

Exercise 2

Take turns practicing asking the questions in Pronunciation Exercise 1 with your partner. Can you input the correct stress pattern?

Exercise 3

Now ask and answer the questions from Warm-up Exercise 3 and Pronunciation Exercise 1 with another partner. Use "Read, Remember, Repeat."

❸ Model Conversation

Exercise 1

🎧23 **Miki is talking to John, who has not lived in Japan long.**

Listen and read the conversation. Then practice the conversation with your partner.

> ⌒ Model Conversation ⌒
>
> Miki: Have you ever ①tried any unusual ②sports?
>
> John: Yes, I ③tried a bungee jump last ④summer.
>
> What about you?
>
> Miki: Well, we're going to ⑤go white-water
>
> rafting this weekend. Do you want to come?
>
> John: Sure, I'd love to.

Exercise 2

Substitute the underlined parts in the model conversation. Start by reading the conversation directly and substituting. Try to only look at the substitution part by the last time.

A	B	C
① eaten	① been to	① had
② food	② festivals	② experiences
③ ate grilled eel	③ went to the *hadaka*	③ tried skydiving
④ month	*matsuri*	④ vacation
⑤ make *mochi*	④ winter	⑤ a hot spring resort
	⑤ watch the *hi-matsuri*	

4 Grammar Exercises

Exercise 1

Match the correct form of the verbs below to the sentences. Then match the sentences to the most natural reply.

be (to)	cook	have	lose	play
read	ride	see	study	write

1. Have you ever _____ a Harry Potter book? ( )

2. Have you ever _____ a famous person? ( )

3. Have you ever _____ a foreign country? ( )

4. Have you ever _____ another foreign language? ( )

5. Have you ever _____ *yakisoba*? ( )

6. Have you ever _____ an accident? ( )

7. Have you ever _____ a motorbike? ( )

8. Have you ever _____ soccer? ( )

9. Have you ever _____ a letter? ( )

10. Have you ever _____ your wallet? ( )

a) No. I only send messages online.

b) Yes, I studied Chinese last year.

c) Yes, I fell off my bicycle last month.

d) Yes, of course. I was in the soccer club at school.

e) Yes, I've seen some famous soccer players.

f) No, but I love the movies.

g) Yes, I once dropped it on the train.

h) No, but I will go to Korea in the vacation.

i) Yes, it's easy to make.

j) No. I think it's a little dangerous.

Exercise 2

Complete the following story with the correct verb in its correct form from the list below.

will enjoy	enjoyed	have been	has been	have never been
will go	went	have studied	have never studied	am going to study

My Summer Homestay Plan

Next summer I _____ to Canada. I _____ to the U.S. before, but I _____ to Canada, so I'm looking forward to it. Actually, my brother _____ to Canada. He _____ to Vancouver two years ago and really _____ it. I _____ English there. Of course, I _____ in Japan for many years, but I _____ abroad before, so I'm sure I _____ it very much.

❺ Pair Dictation

Student A: Turn to page 100.　　　　**Student B: Turn to page 108.**

❶ Vocabulary Review

Exercise **1**

🎧 **24** **David Jones is really into adventure sports. Listen to the talk about his exciting life and check (✓) the extreme things he has done. Put a cross (×) next to the things he has not done yet.** デビッド・ジョーンズはアドベンチャースポーツにはまっています。彼の刺激的な人生体験を聞いて、彼がおこなったことのある過激なスポーツに✓をつけなさい。未経験のスポーツには×をつけなさい。

Adventure Sports	(✓/×)	Where	Ranking
1. bungee jumping	( )		
2. heli-skiing	( )		
3. kayaking	( )		
4. triathlon	( )		
5. white-water rafting	( )		

Exercise **2**

Listen again and write down the name of the places where he tried these sports and rank them in the probable order in which he enjoyed them (1st, 2nd, 3rd…). もう一度聞いて、彼がこれらのスポーツをおこなった場所を記入して、彼が楽しんだと思われる順に、1st、2nd、3rdと番号をつけなさい。

Exercise **3**

Compare with a partner, then take turns explaining about David's adventure sports.

❷ Personalized Conversation

Exercise 1

Change the verb into its past participle to make the opening question. Then think of a suitable follow-up question. Opening Questionの欄に、カッコ内の動詞を過去分詞にして、相手にたずねるYes/No疑問文を作って書きなさい。**Follow-up Question**の欄に、最初の質問に続くWH疑問文を考えて書きなさい。

e.g.　Opening question:　Have you ever been abroad?
　　　Follow-up question:　Where did you go?

Find someone who has done these things:		
Opening Question	Follow-up Question	Name
1. _____ abroad?（be）	Q: _____? A: _____	
2. _____ something unusual?（eat）	Q: _____? A: _____	
3. _____ a bone?（break）	Q: _____? A: _____	
4. _____ someone famous?（meet）	Q: _____? A: _____	
5. _____ in a helicopter?（fly）	Q: _____? A: _____	
6. _____ a ghost?（see）	Q: _____? A: _____	
7. _____ your wallet?（lose）	Q: _____? A: _____	
8. _____ a World Heritage site?（visit）	Q: _____? A: _____	
9. _____ yoga?（do）	Q: _____? A: _____	
10. _____ class?（skip）	Q: _____? A: _____	

Exercise 2

Find out what interesting things your classmates have done.

Rules: You can only write a student who answers, "yes" to the first question.

You can only write a student's name once.

You must form a pair and ask each other, not in a group.

Hints: You should only use English, so use **"Key Point Shadowing"** and **Classroom English** to help you communicate.

Exercise 3

Tell your partner the most interesting thing you found out.

❸ Listening: Model Speech

 Listen and read Aya's speech about her hobby.

Model Speech

My Hobby

What do you like to do in your free time? I'm really into sports, but my hobby is not playing sports or even just watching sports. My hobby is visiting sports stadiums. My hobby is not as usual as other people's hobbies.

I have been to most of the famous soccer and baseball stadiums in Japan. I like to watch sports games, but I also like to visit the stadiums and take pictures of them. I put the pictures on social media like Instagram. Some of them are very beautiful and impressive. The Olympic Stadium in Tokyo is fantastic!

My hobby can be a little expensive because I have to travel far. Last summer I visited Sapporo Dome for the first time. I started this hobby about two years ago. I was watching a baseball game at Koshien and started thinking about visiting other famous places. I have never been abroad, but my dream is to visit famous stadiums around the world like Yankee Stadium in New York or Wembley Stadium in London, so I have to save a lot of money!

④ Personalized Speech

Write a speech about your hobby.

_____

_____

_____

_____

_____

_____

_____

_____

_____

_____

⑤ Speech: Pair Discussion

Exercise 1

Now work in pairs. Read your speech to your conversation partner. Listen carefully to your partner's speech.

Exercise 2

Ask your partner questions. First, write 3 follow-up questions.

Examples of questions:

When did you (first) start _____?

How often do you _____?

Have you ever _____?

MY QUESTIONS

1. _____?

2. _____?

3. _____?

|Exercise 3 ————————————————————————

Now ask your questions.

|Exercise 4 ————————————————————————

Take two minutes to memorize your speech. Then, close the textbook and try to make the speech again. (It is not important to repeat your speech perfectly, just try to remember as much as you can!)

Unit 5

Is it much bigger than Japan?

Part A

1 Warm Up: Key Vocabulary

Exercise 1

Which of the following nouns apply mostly to *urban* or *rural* areas?

次の名詞は都会と田舎のどちらの地域に主に当てはまりますか、下の表に書き込みなさい。

countryside	tall buildings	nature	traffic
museums	entertainment	nightlife	outdoor activities
pollution	rice fields	mountains	parks factories
public transportation		movie complexes	forests
lakes TV tower		radio stations	farms

urban	rural

Look at the example sentences, then write similar sentences describing where you live, using words from above or your own ideas.

(27) e.g. I come from an urban area.   I come from a rural area.

There are many factories.   There aren't any tall buildings.

There is a lot of pollution.   There isn't much nightlife.

1. _____ .

2. _____ .

3. _____ .

4. _____ .

5. _____ .

Language Note

Typically, nouns can also be separated into countable and uncountable. When used to describe general situations, countable nouns are used in the plural form, uncountable nouns in the singular.

e.g.   There **are many** rice fields.   There **is much** more pollution.

名詞の特徴の1つとして、加算名詞と不加算名詞に分けられます。一般的な状況を述べる時には、可算名詞は複数形で、不加算名詞は単数形で使われます。

例）There **are many** rice fields.   There **is much** more pollution.

　　（多くの田んぼがある。）　　　　　（ずっと多くの公害がある。）

Exercise **3**

Read your sentences to your partner. Try to remember what your partner says. Use "Key Point Shadowing" to help.

e.g. A: I come from a rural area.   B: Rural.
      A: There are many mountains.   B: Mountains.
      A: There isn't much entertainment.   B: Entertainment.

Exercise **4**

Change partners and tell your new partner about where your previous partner comes from.

❷ Pronunciation

Exercise **1**

Listen to how the words are linked in the following sentences.

There are a lot of people.	→	The**Ra Ra** lo**T of** people.
There are many people.	→	The**Ra** many people.
There aren't many people.	→	The**Raren't** many people.
There aren't any people.	→	The**Raren'T any** people.

There's a lot of traffic.	→	There'**Za loT of** traffic.
There isn't much traffic.	→	The**Risn't** much traffic.
There isn't any traffic.	→	The**Risn'T any** traffic.

📖 Language Note

The sentence *There is much traffic* sounds too formal for everyday conversation.
There is too much traffic or *There is much more traffic* are fine, though.

*There is much traffic.*という文は日常の会話では堅苦しく聞こえます。ただし、*There is too much traffic.* や *There is much more traffic.*であればかまいません。

Exercise 2

Listen to the sentences again. Note how the stress shifts from the quantifiers, *many, much, any* to the negative form of the *be* verb in the negative statements.

もう一度聞きなさい。否定文では、強勢がmany, much, anyなどの数量を表す語からbe動詞の否定形に移動することに注意しましょう。

Exercise 3

Take turns practicing reading the sentences. Be careful with the linked words and shifting sentence stress.

Exercise 4

Using what you have learned, change partners and tell each other about where you come from (Warm-up Exercise 2).

❸ Model Conversation

Exercise **1**

Tony and Junko are talking about Australia.

Listen and read the conversation. Then practice the conversation with your partner.

Model Conversation

Tony :　Have you ever been to ①Australia?

Junko:　Yes, I have. I went there ②two years ago.

Tony :　What's it like?

Junko:　It's ③much bigger than ④Japan, *but* there aren't as many ⑤people.

Tony :　I'd love to go.

Exercise **2**

Substitute the underlined parts in the model conversation and change the *italic* part where necessary. Start by reading the conversation directly and substituting. Try to only look at the substitution part by the last time.

イタリック体の*but*は必要に応じて変えなさい。

A	B	C
① Shikoku	① Nagano	① Europe
② when I was 13	② when I was in high school	② after I graduated
③ much more relaxed	③ much smaller	③ much older
④ Honshu	④ Tokyo	④ Australia
⑤ jobs	⑤ things to do	⑤ wild animals

# ◆4 Grammar Exercises

Exercise 1

A) Change the following comparative sentences to *not as~ as~* sentences.

e.g.   Tokyo is bigger than Osaka.
        Osaka is not as big as Tokyo.

1. Okinawa is hotter than Hokkaido.

_____ .

2. The Skytree is taller than the Tokyo Tower.

_____ .

3. The Shinkansen is more expensive than the regular train.

_____ .

4. Soccer is more popular than rugby.

_____ .

5. The first movie was better than the second one.

_____ .

B) Write original sentences. (You may include your opinion.) Use a different adjective for each sentence.

e.g.   Skiing is not as exciting as snowboarding.

1. _____ .

2. _____ .

3. _____ .

4. _____ .

5. _____ .

Exercise 2

A) Write original sentences comparing the two words. You may use *-er/more than~* or *not as~as~*. Use a different adjective for each sentence.

e.g. （Osaka / Nagoya）
　　　Osaka is bigger than Nagoya. / Nagoya is not as big as Osaka.

1. _____.
　（spring / fall）

2. _____.
　（soccer / baseball）

3. _____.
　（Japan / the U.S.A.）

4. _____.
　（science / English）

5. _____.
　（I / my friend）

B) Circle the correct word and complete the sentences with your own ideas.

e.g. There *is / are* many beautiful buildings in Tokyo.

1. There *is / are* some interesting places to see in _____.

2. There *is / are* a lot of beautiful nature in _____.

3. There *is / are* exciting nightlife in _____.

4. In my hometown there *isn't / aren't* as many people as in _____.

5. There *is / are* a lot of snow in _____.

5 Pair Dictation

Student A: Turn to page 101.　　　Student B: Turn to page 109.

1 Vocabulary Review

Exercise 1

(30) Ami has just returned from a business trip to New York City and Los Angeles. Listen to her explain about her trip to Hiroyuki. How does she describe the differences between the cities? Make notes.

	New York City	Los Angeles (L.A.)
Differences		
Similarities		

Exercise 2

Listen again. How does she describe the similarities?

Exercise 3

Can you write five sentences describing either differences or similarities between New York City and Los Angeles?

1. _____
2. _____
3. _____
4. _____
5. _____

2 Personalized Conversation

Exercise 1

Think of either a city or a country. Write five sentences describing it, but do not mention its name. Try to include two comparative sentences. You may use your smartphone, but do not forget to ask your teacher first. 1つの国か都市を思い浮かべて、その特徴を表す5つの文を書きなさい。しかし、その名前を言ってはいけません。比較する文を2つ含めるようにしなさい。スマートフォンを使用してもかまいませんが、その前に先生の許可を得ることを忘れないようにしましょう。

e.g.　1. It is a country.

　　　2. It is a continent.

　　　3. It is much bigger than Japan.

　　　4. It is famous for cute animals.

　　　5. There are not as many people in this country as Japan.

1. _____
2. _____
3. _____
4. _____
5. _____

Now, read your sentences to your partner. Can he / she guess what city or country you are describing?

Exercise 2

Change partners and read your sentences to your partner. Can they guess what city or country you are describing?

Exercise 3

Change partners again. Play the game *again*, thinking of *another* city or country.

❸ Listening: Model Speech

(31) **Listen and read Ryusei's speech about his hometown.**

Model Speech

My Hometown

Have you ever heard of Himeji? It is my hometown. Actually, my hometown is famous in Japan, but not so famous abroad.

Himeji is located in Hyogo Prefecture in the Kansai area of Japan. On the Shinkansen it is between Osaka and Okayama. The population is about 500,000.

The most famous place in Himeji is Himeji Castle. (This is called Himeji-jo in Japanese.) I think it is the most impressive castle in Japan. It is very large and the traditional Japanese gardens are very beautiful. There are also some interesting museums near the castle.

Himeji is not as big or famous as Osaka or Kyoto. There aren't as many restaurants and there isn't as much nightlife, but it is an interesting place to visit and has a lot of history, so I am very proud of my hometown. In the future, I might work and live in a bigger city, but I will always be proud of Himeji!

4 Personalized Speech

Write a speech about your hometown.

_____

_____

_____

_____

_____

_____

_____

_____

_____

_____

_____

5 Speech: Pair Discussion

Exercise 1

Now work in pairs. Read your speech to your conversation partner. Listen carefully to your partner's speech.

Exercise 2

Ask your partner questions. First, write 3 follow-up questions.

Examples of questions:

Are there any _____ in your hometown?

Do you want to live in your hometown in the future?

Tell me more about _____.

MY QUESTIONS

1. _____ ?

2. _____ ?

3. _____ ?

Exercise 3

Now ask your questions.

Exercise 4

Take two minutes to memorize your speech. Then, close the textbook and try to make the speech again. (It is not important to repeat your speech perfectly, just try to remember as much as you can!)

Are you ready to order?

1 Warm Up: Key Vocabulary

Exercise 1

The following are some of the rules about countable and uncountable nouns. With your partner complete these rules, using the words countable, uncountable or both. 次の文は、加算名詞と不加算名詞に関する規則です。空所にcountable, uncountable, both のどれを入れるのがよいかをペアで相談し、規則を完成しなさい。

1. When more than one is eaten, the food is _____.
　e.g.　carrots, beans

2. Food that is a liquid（or was a liquid at the time of making）is _____.
　e.g.　yogurt, cheese

3. Food that is not eaten whole is _____.
　e.g.　meat, pork

4. Food that can be eaten whole or not can be _____.
　e.g.　pizza, chocolate, ice cream（cone）

5. Food that is too numerous to count is either _____ or
　_____, but not _____.
　e.g.　noodles, rice

6. The word *vegetable* is _____, but the word *fruit* is
　_____.

Exercise 2

Separate the food in the box below into countable, uncountable or both.

spaghetti	bread	yogurt	noodles	pork	chicken	peanuts
meat	soup	pizza	potatoes	cheese	fish	cherries
carrots	beans	rice	cake	chocolate	pie	beef

countable	uncountable	both

Exercise 3

Prepare answers for the following questions.

1. What's your favorite food?

_____

2. How often do you eat it?

_____

3. When was the last time you ate it?

_____

4. Where did you eat it?

_____

5. What was it like?

_____

Now ask and answer about your favorite food.

Exercise 4

Now take turns interviewing a new partner about their favorite food. Try not to look at your answers when it is your turn to answer questions.

❷ Pronunciation

Exercise 1

Predict the correct stress patterns for the questions in Warm Up Exercise 3 by writing a ✓ in the ( ) .

1.	Whát's your fávorite fóod? ( )	Whát's yóur favorite fóod? ( )
2.	Hów often dó you eat ít? ( )	How óften do you éat it? ( )
3.	Whén was the lást time you áte it? ( )	Whén was the lást tíme you áte it? ( )
4.	Whére did you éat it? ( )	Whére díd you eat ít? ( )
5.	Whát wás it líke? ( )	Whát was it líke? ( )

Exercise 2

Now listen and check your predictions. Then ask your partner these questions.

Exercise 3

Memorize the questions then interview another partner, taking care of the stress patterns.

❸ Model Conversation

| Exercise 1 ──────────────────────────────────

🎧35 **A mother is serving her child dinner.**
Listen and read the conversation. Then practice the conversation with your partner.

> Model Conversation
>
> Mother: Would you like some ①fish?
>
> Child : Only ②a little, please.
>
> Mother: How about ③vegetables? How ④many would you like?
>
> Child : Not ④many. I'm not keen on *them*.
>
> Mother: Okay. Well, enjoy your meal.

| Exercise 2 ──────────────────────────────────

Substitute the underlined parts in the model conversation and change the italic *them* to *it* where necessary. Start by reading the conversation directly and substituting. Try to only look at the substitution part by the last time.

A	B	C
① noodles	① pie	① meat
② a few	② a little	② a little
③ soup	③ ice cream	③ potatoes
④ much	④ much	④ many

Language Note ─────────────────────────

Beginner learners of English learn that **some** is used in positive sentences and **any** is used in negative sentences or questions. However, **some** is also used for questions that are offers or questions where the speaker expects the answer to be 'Yes'.

someは肯定文に、anyは否定文や疑問文に使用されると英語学習の初期段階で学びます。しかし、肯定（Yes）の答えを期待してたずねる時や提案する場合には、疑問文にもsome が使われます。

④ Grammar Exercises

Exercise 1

Circle the correct word in each sentence.

1. There's *some / any* cheese in the fridge if you're hungry.
2. We don't have *some / any* bread. I'll buy *some / any*.
3. Can I have *some / any* more rice, please?
4. How *many / much* sausages do you want?
5. How *many / much* soy sauce do you want?
6. I'd like *some / any* bread, please.
7. Did he drink *many / a lot of* beer last night?
8. Did he drink *many / much* bottles of beer last night?
9. It's too expensive. I don't have *many / much* money.

Exercise 2

Match the expressions on the left with the food or drink items on the right. (More than one answer is possible.)

1. a bag of   ·   · eggs
2. a loaf of   ·   · coke
3. a jar of   ·   · pizza
4. a box of   ·   · rice
5. a can of   ·   · bread
6. a bottle of   ·   · jam
7. a carton of ·   · wine
8. a slice of   ·   · chocolates

⑤ Pair Dictation

Student A: Turn to page 102.   **Student B: Turn to page 110.**

➊ Vocabulary Review

Exercise 1

(36) Todd and Krystal are deciding what to do for dinner. Read the statements, then listen to the conversation and mark each statement T for true or F for false.

1. Krystal does not want to cook dinner.   (   )
2. They probably ordered pizza last week.   (   )
3. The new pizza place is called Derek's.   (   )
4. Luigi's is a little cheaper than Derek's.   (   )
5. Luigi's deliveries are faster than Derek's.   (   )
6. They have probably tried Derek's pizzas before.   (   )
7. They decide to order one pizza.   (   )
8. Krystal orders the spicy chicken pizza.   (   )

Exercise 2

Listen again and correct the false statements.

Exercise 3

Read the correct statements again. Now change your partner and practice telling the story to each other without looking at your textbooks. The listener should check whether the speaker is telling the story correctly.

2 Personalized Conversation

Exercise 1

On your own, read the two conversations to yourself. Compare the style of language and then read the Language Note. 次の2種類の会話を黙読して、表現の違いを観察しなさい。その後で、Language Noteの解説を読みなさい。

At a fast-food restaurant

Server:	Are you ready to order?
Customer:	Yes, I want a double cheeseburger, please.
Server:	To eat in or take away?
Customer:	Err... Eat in.
Server:	Do you want anything to drink?
Customer:	Yes, a coke, please.
Server:	We have small, medium or large.
Customer:	A large, please.
Server:	Do you want anything else?
Customer:	No, thanks.
Server:	So, that's one double cheeseburger and a large coke. That'll be $3.50.
Customer:	Here's $5.
Server:	And $1.50 change. Enjoy your meal.
Customer:	Thanks.

At a restaurant

Server:	Can I take your order?
Customer:	Yes, I'd like the salmon, please.
Server:	That's fine. And would you like a starter?
Customer:	Umm... No, I don't think so.
Server:	How about a dessert?
Customer:	Yes, I'll have the chocolate cake.
Server:	Would you like some ice cream with that?
Customer:	No, thank you.
Server:	And would you like anything to drink?
Customer:	Yes, I'd like a sparkling water, please.
Server:	Okay then. Your meal will be with you soon.
Customer:	Thank you very much.

 Language Note

In restaurants it is more polite to use *would like* than *want*. The word *want* is acceptable in fast-food restaurants or among friends and family.

レストランでは、*want* より*would like*を使用する方がていねいです。ファーストフードレストランの場合や、友人、家族の間では*want*でも大丈夫です。

In restaurants people often ask for *the* beef or *the* chicken rather than *some* beef or *some* chicken. This is slightly more formal and refers to the chicken or beef dish on the menu.

レストランでは、*some* beef あるいは *some* chickenよりも*the* beef あるいは *the* chickenと言って注文します。この言い方は多少形式ばっていますが、*the*を用いるのはメニューのチキンや肉料理を指しているからです。

Always use *please* or *thank you* when ordering food, even if you forget the correct grammatical English. Not to do so sounds very rude.

文法的に正しい英語をたとえ忘れても、食べ物を注文する時にはいつも*please* あるいは *thank you*を加えましょう。そうでないと、とても失礼に響きます。

Exercise 2

Look at the menus below. In pairs, role-play ordering food at both types of restaurant. Take turns being the server.

At a fast-food restaurant

Bob's Burgers			large	medium	small
Hamburger	$1.50				
Cheeseburger	$2.00	fries	$1.00	$0.75	$0.50
Double Cheeseburger	$2.50	coke	$1.00	$0.75	$0.50
Teriyaki Burger	$2.75	juice	$1.25	$1.00	$0.75
Filet o' Fish Burger	$2.25	tea	$1.50	$1.25	$1.00
Beanburger	$2.00	coffee	$1.50	$1.25	$1.00

At a restaurant

Ben's Bistro

Starter	Main *	Dessert
❖ Chef's Salad	❖ Roast Beef	❖ Fruit Tart
❖ Squid Rings	❖ Barbecue Pork	❖ Chocolate Cake
❖ Tomato Soup	❖ Grilled Chicken	❖ Ice Cream
	❖ Salmon	**Drink**
	❖ Spaghetti	❖ Sparkling Water
	❖ Vegan Quiche	❖ Coke
		❖ Tea
		❖ Juice, orange / apple

* All mains are served with either salad and fries, or seasonal vegetables.

Exercise 3

Change partners and role-play the two situations again. This time try not to read the conversations. You may look at the menus, of course!

❸ Listening: Model Speech

 Listen and read Momo's speech about her favorite restaurant.

(Model Speech)

My Favorite Restaurant

My favorite restaurant is actually a coffee shop called Sakura. It is near my house. I think it first opened about ten years ago. It is not a chain restaurant.

It is a coffee shop and restaurant. You don't have to eat there. You can just have a drink if you like, but there is a good menu with some set meals and snacks. The cakes are delicious!

My favorite meal is the spaghetti lunch. The food is not so expensive, so you don't have to spend a lot of money there. For example, lunch is from ¥700 to ¥900, including a drink.

It is not such a big place. There is a counter and maybe four or five tables. Also, the owner and staff are very friendly. It is very relaxing and a good place to hang out with friends. Sakura is open almost every day, including national holidays. However, it is closed on Wednesdays. The opening hours are from 11 a.m. to 9 p.m.

Please come with me to Sakura sometime.

❹ Personalized Speech

Write a speech about your favorite restaurant, cafe or coffee shop.

⑤ Speech: Pair Discussion

Exercise 1

Now work in pairs. Read your speech to your conversation partner. Listen carefully to your partner's speech.

Exercise 2

Ask your partner questions. First, write 3 follow-up questions.

Examples of questions:

How often do you go there?

Do they have / sell _____?

How do I get there?

MY QUESTIONS

1. _____ ?

2. _____ ?

3. _____ ?

Exercise 3

Now ask your questions.

Exercise 4

Take two minutes to memorize your speech. Then, close the textbook and try to make the speech again. (It is not important to repeat your speech perfectly, just try to remember as much as you can!)

Warm-up
Unit 1
Unit 2
Unit 3
Review 1
Unit 4
Unit 5
Unit 6
Review 2

❶ Interview Test questions

Answer the questions about yourself with complete sentences.

When answering yes or no, give reasons or examples. Yes, Noで答える時には、その理由や例を付け加えましょう。

1. Have you ever been abroad?

_____

2. Have you ever eaten any unusual food?

_____

3. Are you into dangerous sports?

_____

4. What is the most exciting thing you have ever done?

_____

5. Do you live in an urban or rural area?

_____

6. Write two sentences about where you live:

1) _____

2) _____

7. Do you like your neighborhood?

_____

8. What's your favorite dish?

_____

9. How often do you eat it?

_____

10. When was the last time you ate it?

_____

11. Where did you eat it?

_____

❷ Grammar

Circle the correct word(s).

1. There _____ many beautiful beaches in Brazil.
   [is / are / was]

2. I have never _____ Thai food.
   [eat / ate / eaten]

3. Which is _____, Paris or London?
   [big / bigger / biggest]

4. Summer is _____ than spring.
   [hot / more hot / hotter]

5. There is _____ pollution in my hometown.
   [a lot of / many / any]

6. Have you ever _____ a ghost?
   [see / saw / seen]

7. Osaka is not _____ as Tokyo.
   [big / as big / bigger]

8. Can I have _____ cup of coffee, please?
   [a / some / any]

❸ Vocabulary

Write the words in the correct spaces. (Change to plural if necessary.)

factory	museum	online	pollution
population	rice field	spaghetti	transportation

1. I love Italian food, especially _____.

2. The _____ of Japan is over 120 million.

3. You can book a ticket _____.

4. When we visited Paris, we went to many wonderful _____.

5. The air is a little dirty. There is too much _____.

Warm-up
Unit 1
Unit 2
Unit 3
Review 1
Unit 4
Unit 5
Unit 6
Review 2

6. I live in the countryside. There is nothing near my house, only _____.

7. You don't need a car in this city. The public _____ is excellent.

8. She works for Toyota in a car _____.

4 Writing I

Write the sentences in the correct order.

1. been / Hawaii / never / he / has / to

_____.

2. more / Niigata / famous / than / is / Kyoto

_____.

3. many / are / there / museums / London / in

_____.

4. please / a steak / I'd / like

_____.

5. been / you / to / ever / have / Sapporo

_____?

6. as / as / not / Keiko / tall / is / sister / her

_____.

7. Japanese / English / is / which / difficult / more / or

_____?

8. the / his / tallest / class / John / is / in

_____.

⑤ Writing II

Write a question that matches each answer. (There may be more than one correct question.)

1. A: _____?

B: Yes, I have. I've been to Korea, Hong Kong and Guam.

2. A: _____?

B: Soccer or rugby? I think soccer is more popular.

3. A: _____?

B: I was born in Nagano, but I grew up in Tokyo.

4. A: _____?

B: My part-time job? I started it last year.

5. A: _____?

B: My hometown? It's very quiet and has a lot of beautiful nature.

6. A: _____?

B: No, I haven't. I can ski, but I've never tried snowboarding.

7. A: _____?

B: Yes, I'd like a hamburger, please.

8. A: _____?

B: Nagoya? I think it's over two million.

9. A: _____?

B: It's open from 5 p.m. to 11 p.m.

10. A: _____?

B: Yes, I'd like an orange juice, please.

6 Comprehension

Read the conversation about Kazunori's trip to Bali. Then answer the questions with full sentences.

(41)

Michael :	So, how was Bali?
Kazunori:	It was fantastic, thank you.
Michael :	I hear it's a very interesting place.
Kazunori:	Yes, it has a unique culture and there is a lot of beautiful nature.
Michael :	What did you do there?
Kazunori:	Well, we stayed at the beach and went scuba diving a few times. Have you ever tried it?
Michael :	Once, but I didn't like it. What about the mountains? Did you go there?
Kazunori:	Yes, we visited a temple in the mountains and there were many rice fields. The view was amazing.
Michael :	What was the food like?
Kazunori:	My favorite dish was *nasi goreng*. You eat it for breakfast.
Michael :	*Nasi goreng?* What's that?
Kazunori:	It's fried rice with a little salad and a fried egg. It's delicious.
Michael :	Tell me more about the culture.
Kazunori:	Well, the music is wonderful and there are many dances. We watched a wonderful performance.
Michael :	It sounds like you had a great time.
Kazunori:	Yes, Bali is much more relaxing than Japan. I'd like to visit again.

1. Did Kazunori enjoy his trip to Bali?

_____

2. Why is Bali interesting?

_____

3. Has Michael ever tried scuba diving?

_____

4. What did Kazunori do in the mountains?

_____

5. What was the view like?

6. What is *nasi goreng*?

7. When do people eat it?

8. Name two things Kazunori says about the culture.

9. How was the dance performance?

10. How does Kazunori compare Bali to Japan?

11. What would Kazunori like to do again?

12. Would you like to visit Bali one day?

Warm-up

Unit 1

Unit 2

Unit 3

Review 1

Unit 4

Unit 5

Unit 6

Review 2

For student **A**

Unit **1** [Part **A**] ❺ **Pair Dictation** (Page 19)

Exercise **1**

Dictate the following sentences to your partner.

次の英文を読み上げて、パートナーに書き取ってもらいなさい。

> Tom is interested in learning languages. He speaks Japanese very well. He is also good at Korean and he is learning Chinese, too. He likes to study.

Exercise **2**

Now listen and write down what your partner says.

今度はあなたがパートナーの言ったことを書き取りなさい。

_____

_____

_____

_____

_____

Unit 2 [Part A] ⑤ Pair Dictation (Page 30)

Exercise 1

Dictate the following sentences to your partner.

🎧 44

> Sarah's friend is visiting from Australia on Saturday afternoon. She has to do many things by then. She has to hand in her homework by Friday and then she has to clean her room.

Exercise 2

Now listen and write down what your partner says.

_____

_____

_____

_____

_____

Unit **3** [Part **A**] ⑤ **Pair Dictation** (Page 40)

Exercise **1**

Dictate the following sentences to your partner.

🎧46

> There was an earthquake yesterday afternoon. I was working at my part-time job when it happened. I work at an Italian restaurant. We all went under the tables and waited until the earthquake stopped.

Exercise **2**

Now listen and write down what your partner says.

_____

_____

_____

_____

_____

_____

Student A: Witness

Exercise 1 ─────────────────────────────

You witnessed a crime in the picture on next page. Prepare sentences to answer the police officer's questions. Remember the crime happened in the past, so you should use the past tense. あなたは次ページの絵に描かれた犯罪を目撃しました。警察官の質問に対して答えるための準備をしなさい。犯罪は過去に起きたので、過去形を使用することを忘れないようにしましょう。

1. name	
2. occupation	
3. time of the crime	
4. what you were doing	
5. what you saw	
6. what the people were doing	
7. what the people looked like	
8. what the people were wearing	

Exercise 2 ─────────────────────────────

Listen carefully to the police officer's questions and answer with as much detail as you can. 警察官の質問を注深く聞いて、できる限り詳しく答えなさい。

Exercise 3 ─────────────────────────────

Turn back to page 42.

Exercise **1**

Dictate the following sentences to your partner.

(48)

> Stefan has visited many interesting places. He traveled across Vietnam and Cambodia last spring vacation. And this year he is going to South America.

Exercise **2**

Now listen and write down what your partner says.

_____

_____

_____

_____

_____

Unit **5** [Part A] ◆**Pair Dictation** (Page 71)

Exercise **1**

Dictate the following sentences to your partner.

> Steve moved to Tokyo. His new apartment is not as big as his old one, but it is modern. There is much more entertainment in his neighborhood, but it is nosier, too.

Exercise **2**

Now listen and write down what your partner says.

Unit 6 [Part A] 5 Pair Dictation (Page 81)

Exercise 1

Dictate the following sentences to your partner.

Takuma loves rice. He likes it much more than bread or pasta. He eats rice with every meal. He eats two bowls of rice for breakfast and dinner. He usually takes rice balls for lunch, too.

Exercise 2

Now listen and write down what your partner says.

_____

_____

_____

_____

_____

Unit **1** ［Part A］ ⑤ **Pair Dictation** (Page 19)

Exercise **1**

Listen and write down what your partner says.

読み上げられた英文を書き取りなさい。

_____

_____

_____

_____

_____

_____

Exercise **2**

Now dictate the following sentences to your partner.

今度は、あなたが次の英文を読み上げて、書き取ってもらいなさい。

> Tina is an only child. She lives in an apartment with her parents and her dog, Scooby. She takes him for walks and loves to play with him in the park next to her apartment building.

Unit 2 [Part A] ⑤ Pair Dictation (Page 30)

Exercise 1

Listen and write down what your partner says.

_____

_____

_____

_____

_____

_____

Exercise 2

Now dictate the following sentences to your partner.

> Steve is having a busy week. He is meeting his customers tomorrow morning and then he has to go to the dentist. He also has to finish a report by 5:00 p.m. on Friday.

Unit 3 [Part A] ⑤ Pair Dictation (Page 40)

Exercise 1

Listen and write down what your partner says.

_____

_____

_____

_____

_____

_____

Exercise 2

Now dictate the following sentences to your partner.

> I was walking home from school when I saw an accident. A girl was riding a bicycle when a car hit her. She wasn't injured, so I think she was very lucky.

Student B: Police Officer

| Exercise **1**

You are going to interview a witness of a crime in the picture on next page. Prepare questions to ask the witness. Remember the crime happened in the past, so you should use the past tense. あなたは次ページの絵に描かれた犯罪を目撃した人に質問します。目撃者にたずねる質問を準備しなさい。犯罪は過去に起きたので、過去形を使用することを忘れないようにしましょう。

1. name	
2. occupation	
3. time of the crime	
4. what the witness was doing	
5. what the witness saw	
6. what the people were doing	
7. what the people looked like	
8. what the people were wearing	

| Exercise **2**

Make a sketch or write notes in the crime scene above as you listen to the witness' answers to your questions. あなたの質問に対する目撃者の答えを聞いて、絵に描き加えなさい。あるいはメモを取りなさい。

| Exercise **3**

Turn back to page 42.

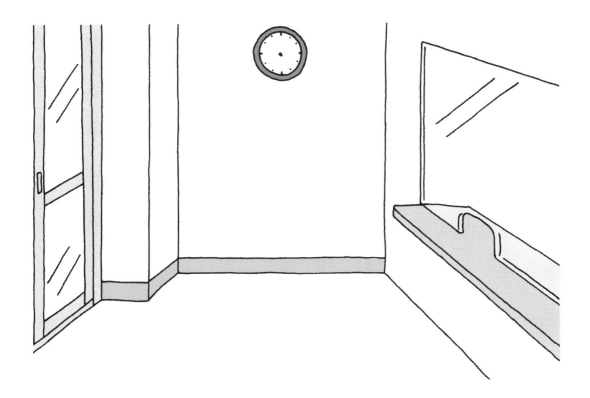

Unit 4 [Part A] ⑤ Pair Dictation (Page 59)

Exercise 1

Listen and write down what your partner says.

_____

_____

_____

_____

_____

_____

Exercise 2

Now dictate the following sentences to your partner.

49

> Maiko is really into dangerous sports. She has tried bungee jumping in New Zealand and has been white-water rafting in Bali. Next, she wants to go skydiving!

Unit **5** [Part A] **⑤ Pair Dictation** (Page 71)

Exercise **1**

Listen and write down what your partner says.

_____

_____

_____

_____

_____

_____

Exercise **2**

Now dictate the following sentences to your partner.

> Judy started to work for a new company in Osaka. There are many more people at this company and the job is more interesting than her old one. The pay is also much better.

| Exercise 1 ───────────────────────────────

Listen and write down what your partner says.

_____

_____

_____

_____

_____

_____

| Exercise 2 ───────────────────────────────

Now dictate the following sentences to your partner.

Martha is keen on pizza. Her family often orders pizzas from a delivery company on Friday nights. They love to eat pizza and watch movies together. She would like to visit Italy and eat real pizza one day.

Glossary for Reception
（理解のための語彙）

本書の英文の内容を理解するのに必要と思われる語彙をアルファベット順に
一覧できるようにしました。意味がわからない時に利用してください。

A

above	上の
abroad	海外へ、海外で
acceptable	受け入れられる、好ましい
accident	事故
actually	実際に、実は
add	加える
adjective	形容詞
adventure	冒険
agree	同意する
aim	目的
amazing	驚くべき、すごい
an only child	一人っ子
apartment	アパート、マンション
arrow	矢印
auxiliary verb	助動詞

B

Bali	バリ
be into 〜	〜にはまっている
be located	位置する
bean	豆
beef	牛肉
below	下の
bistro	ビストロ（小型のレストラン）
blog post	ブログの投稿・記事
board game	ボードゲーム（チェス、オセロなど）
bone	骨
book	予約する
boss	上司
bottle	びん
bowl	茶碗１杯の量
bungee jump(ing)	バンジージャンプ
by oneself	一人で

C

Cambodia	カンボジア
carrot	ニンジン
carton	カートン、紙箱
cash register	レジ
castle	城
casual	略式の、カジュアルな
certain	とある〜
chain	チェーン店
change	お釣り
character	人物
chat	おしゃべりする
cheeseburger	チーズバーガー
Chinese	中国語、中華料理
chore	毎日の仕事、日課
classical music	クラシック音楽
clothes	服装
co-worker	同僚
coke	コーラ
column	欄
commitment	約束、義務
common	普通の、共通の
comparative	比較の
compare	比べる
compare 〜 to ...	〜を…にたとえる
complete	完成する
cone	コーン、円錐形
confuse	混同する
Congratulations!	おめでとう！
consonant	子音
continent	大陸
continue	続ける
correct	正しい
correctly	正しく
Could you 〜?	〜してくれませんか？
countable	加算の
counter	カウンター
craft	手工芸、工芸品
crime	犯罪
cross	Xの印

culture	文化
customer	顧客
cute	かわいい

D

damage	損害を与える、損害
dangerous	危険な
deadline	締め切り
decide	決める
delivery	配達
deluxe	デラックス
dentist	歯医者
department store	デパート
describe	記述する、述べる
dessert	デザート
detail	詳細
dial	ダイアル
dictate	書き取らせる
difference	相違点
directly	直接的に
dirty	汚い
disappointed	がっかりした、落胆して
disaster	災害
discuss	話し合う
dish	料理
draw	描く
drop off	置いていく、出す
duty	義務、任務

E

earthquake	地震
eel	うなぎ
elementary school	小学校
else	他に
embarrassed	困って
engineer	技師
entertainment	娯楽
entrance	入り口、入場
erupt	噴火する
especially	とりわけ、特に
Europe	ヨーロッパ
event	イベント、行事
excellent	ひじょうに優れた、優秀な
experience	経験
explanation	説明
expression	表現

| extreme | 極端な |

F

factory	工場
fall off	落ちる、落っこちる
false	間違った
fantastic	素晴らしい
far	遠くへ、遠くに
farm	農場
fast food	ファーストフード
favorite	大好きな
fill in	記入する
follow	続く
follow-up question	追加質問、関連質問
following	次の
for the first time	初めて
foreign language	外国語
form	結成する、作る
free	無料の
fries	フライドポテト
fridge	冷蔵庫

G

general	一般的な
get to ～	～するようになる
graduate	卒業する
grammatical	文法的な
greet	挨拶する
greeting	挨拶
grill	網焼きにする
grow up	成長する、育つ
guess	推測する、思う

H

hamburger	ハンバーガー
hand in ～	～を提出する
hang out with ～	～とぶらぶらして時を過ごす
happen	起こる
Harry Potter	ハリー・ポッター
have ～ in common	～を共有している
Hawaii	ハワイ
head office	本社、本店
heli-skiing	ヘリスキー
helicopter	ヘリコプター
history	歴史
hit	襲う、当たる

Hong Kong	香港
horror	ホラー（映画）、恐怖もの
hot spring	温泉
hourly pay	時間給

I

ice-skating	アイススケート
identify	結びつける、確認する
impressive	印象的な
in the future	将来
in turn	順番に
include	含む
incorrect	不正確な、誤った
informal	非公式な、形式ばらない
injure	傷つける
input	入れる
Instagram	インスタグラム
instead of ～	～の代わりに
interview	面接する、尋問する
intonation	イントネーション
introduce	紹介する
item	項目

J

jar	1びんの量

K

kayaking	カヤック
keen	熱中して
kind of ～	ちょっと、いくぶん
Korean	韓国の、韓国語、韓国人

L

L.A.	ロサンゼルス（=Los Angeles）
label	ラベルをはる、分類する
language	言語
leg	脚
link	つなぐ
liquid	液体
loaf	パン1個
look around	見物して回る
look for ～	～をさがす
lots	たくさんのこと

M

mahjong	麻雀
main	（コースの）メインの料理
major	専攻
make notes	メモする
match	組み合わせる
medium	中間の
memorize	覚える、暗記する
mention	述べる
menu	メニュー
million	百万
mistake	誤り、間違い
mistakenly	誤って
mobile phone	携帯電話
mostly	たいていの場合、主として
motorbike	バイク、原付自転車
musical instrument	楽器

N

nap	昼寝、うたた寝する
national holiday	国民の祝日
natural	自然な
nature	自然
nearby	近くに
negative	否定の
neighborhood	近隣、近所
New Year's Day	正月、元旦
New Year's Eve	大晦日
night shift	夜間勤務、夜勤
nightlife	夜の娯楽、ナイトライフ
noisy	騒がしい
noodle	麺類
note	注、注目する
noun	名詞
numerous	多数からなる

O

occupation	職業
offer	申し出、提供
on one's own	ひとりで
once	いったん～したら
order	注文（する）、順序
original	独自の
outdoor	戸外の
overtime	時間外の、超過勤務で
owner	オーナー

P

part-time job	アルバイト
past participle	過去分詞
pasta	パスタ
pause	休止する、間を置く
pay	賃金
P.E.	体育（=physical education）
peanut	ピーナツ
perfectly	完璧に
performance	演奏、演技
personalize	自分にあてはめる
phone	電話する
phrase	語句
plain form	（動詞の）原形
plural	複数形（の）
police report	警察の調書、捜査報告
polite	ていねいな
pollution	汚染
population	人口
positive	肯定的な
predict	予測する
prediction	予測
prefecture	県
prefer	好む
prepare	準備する
present continuous	現在進行の、現在進行形
presentation	プレゼン
previous	前の
probable	ありそうな
pronounce	発音する
pronunciation	発音
proud	誇りに思って
public transportation	公共交通

Q

quantifier	数量語
quiche	キッシュ

R

radio station	ラジオ局
raise	あげる
rank	順位をつける
reduced form	弱音形、縮小形
refer	言及する
regular	通常の、普通の
relaxed	のんびりした、くつろいで

replace	置き換える
reply	返答、答える
restaurant	レストラン
review	復習する
rewrite	書き直す
rice ball	おにぎり
rice field	稲田、田んぼ
rob	奪う、強奪する
role	役割
role-play	役割を演ずる
rude	無礼な
rugby	ラグビー
rural	田舎の

S

sales report	売上報告書
salmon	鮭
sausage	ソーセージ
save	貯める
schedule	スケジュール
scuba diving	スキューバダイビング
seasonal	季節の
self-introduction	自己紹介
sentence	文
separate	分離する、分類する
serious	深刻な
server	給仕
set meal	定食
shift	交替、移動する
shorten	短くする
shy	恥ずかしがりの
similar	似ている
similarity	類似点
simple	簡単な
simple present	単純現在（形）
singular	単数形（の）
situation	状況
sketch	略図、スケッチする
skip a class	授業をさぼる
skydiving	スカイダイビング
Skytree	スカイツリー
slice	薄切り1枚
slightly	少し
snack	軽食
snowboarding	スノーボード
So do I.	私もそうです。

social media	ソーシャルメディア
sound like ～	～ように思われる、聞こえる
soy sauce	醤油
spaghetti	スパゲティ
sparkling	発泡性の
spicy	香辛料を入れた
squid	イカ
stadium	スタジアム、競技場
staff	スタッフ、店員
starter	最初の料理
statement	記述、発言、文
steak	ステーキ
stress	強勢
stress mark	アクセント符号
substitute	置き換える
subway	地下鉄
suitable	適した
support	支持する

T

table	表
take away	持ち帰る
take notes	メモを取る
take out	持ち出す、取り出す
take turns	交替でする
tart	タルト
tense	時制
terrible	ひどい、恐ろしい
Thai	タイの
third person	三人称
tidy	きれいにする
traditional	伝統的な
traffic	交通
trash	ごみ
triathlon	トライアスロン
turn to page ～	～ページを開く
tutor	指導教員、チューター
twice	2回、2倍
typhoon	台風
typical	典型的な
typically	典型的に、主として

U

uncountable	不可算の
underline	下線を施す
uniform	制服
unique	独特の、ユニークな
unscramble	正しく並べ替える
unusual	珍しい、まれな
urban	都会の
usually	通常は、普通は

V

Vancouver	バンクーバー
vegan	極端な採食主義者
vegetable	野菜
verb	動詞
version	～版
Vietnam	ベトナム
view	景色
vocabulary	語彙
volcano	火山
vowel	母音

W

wallet	財布
Wembley	ウェンブリー（ロンドン郊外の北西部にある町）
while	一方
white-water rafting	急流下り
whole	丸ごと
wild	野生の
witness	目撃する、目撃者
work from home	自宅で働く、在宅で勤務する
World Heritage (site)	世界遺産
worried	心配して
worry	心配する
wow	うわー！すごい！
wrestle	取っ組み合う
wrestler	レスリング選手

Y

yoga	ヨガ
yogurt	ヨーグルト

Z

Zambezi	ザンベジ川（アフリカ南部を流れインド洋に注ぐ）

Glossary for Production
（発話のための語彙）

ペアで活動する際に役立つと思われる語彙について、トピック別にアイウエオ順にまとめてみました。日本語に相当する英語がわからない時に活用してください。

1 アルバイト（Part-time Jobs）
（1）職種（Types of Jobs）

〜員	〜 worker
インストラクター	instructor
ウェイター	waiter / server
ウェイトレス	waitress / server
受付係	receptionist
家庭教師	tutor
教師	teacher
スタッフ	member of staff
清掃係	cleaner
調理係	cook
店員	clerk, salesperson
配達係	deliverer
レジ係	cashier

（2）アルバイト先（Workplaces）

学習塾	cram school / juku
ガソリンスタンド	gas station
結婚式場	wedding hall
工場	factory
コンサートホール	concert hall
コンビニ	convenience store
食料雑貨店	grocery store
書店	bookshop
ジム	gym
スーパー	supermarket
スポーツ・センター	sports center
倉庫	warehouse
デパート	department store
〜店	〜 store / shop
花屋	flower shop
バー	bar
100円ショップ	100-yen shop
郵便局	post office

（3）その他（Other）

客	customer
給仕する	serve
勤務時間	working hours
勤務条件	working conditions
経験	experience
仕事を探す	look for a job
仕事を辞める	quit a job
時間給	hourly pay / wage
掃除する	clean
将来役立つ	(be) useful for the future
職務	duties
上司	boss
制服	uniform
注文を取る	take orders
賃金	pay / salary
同僚	co-worker
〜 の責任がある	(be) responsible for 〜
（〜から〜まで）働く	work from 〜 to / until 〜
バイトがある	have a part-time job
まかない料理	free food / meals
マネージャー	manager
面接	interview
良い経験になる	(be) a good experience

2 余暇の活動・趣味・娯楽
（Leisure Activities, Hobbies, Pastimes）
（1）名詞（Nouns）

アニメ	animation
編物	knitting
インターネット	the Internet
ウェート・トレーニング	weight training
エアロビクス	aerobics
絵画	painting
格闘技	martial arts
カラオケ	singing karaoke

楽器	musical instrument
切手収集	stamp collecting
キャンプ	camping
ギャンブル	gambling
弓道	Japanese archery
コンピューターおたく	computer freak
サーフィン	surfing
サイクリング	cycling
魚釣り	fishing
小説	novel
ジョギング	jogging
推理小説	mystery
スキー	skiing
スケート	skating
スケボー	skateboarding
スノーボード	snowboarding
ダイビング	diving
ドライブ	driving
ハイキング	hiking
ビデオゲーム	video games
ボードゲーム	board games
ボーリング	bowling
漫画	comic
ヨット遊び	sailing
料理	cooking

(2) 動詞 (Verbs)

(〜を)集める	collect 〜
インターネット・サーフィンする	surf the Internet / the net
絵を描く	draw / paint
(楽器を)演奏する	play (musical instrument)
オンランで投稿する	post online
(〜を)鑑賞する、観る	watch 〜
(〜に)興味がある	(be) interested in 〜
〜しに行く	go 〜ing
(スポーツを)する	play (sports)
(格闘技を)する	do (martial arts)
(〜が)大好き	love 〜
読書する	read
〜の世話をする	look after 〜
(〜に)乗る	ride 〜
走る	run
(〜に)はまっている	(be) into 〜 / keen on 〜
勉強する	study

3 故郷 (Hometown)
(1) 様々な場所 (Places in Town)

駅	station
空港	airport
公園	park
城	castle
建物	building
庭園	garden
通り	street / road
博物館	museum
美術館	art gallery

(2) その他 (Other)

(〜に)位置している	(be) located in 〜
気候	climate
交通	transportation
娯楽	entertainment
人口	population
スポーツチーム	sports team
生活スタイル	lifestyle
ナイトライフ	nightlife
祭り	festival
土産	souvenir
名物(料理)	local food / dish
(〜で)有名な	(be) famous for 〜

4 食べ物 (Food)
(1) 野菜と果物 (Fruit and Vegetables)

アスパラガス	asparagus
苺	strawberry
オレンジ	orange
カブ	turnip
かぼちゃ	pumpkin
カリフラワー	cauliflower
きゅうり	cucumber
グレープフルーツ	grapefruit
さくらんぼ	cherry
じゃがいも	potato
スイカ	watermelon
セロリ	celery
玉ねぎ	onion
とうもろこし	corn
トマト	tomato
ナシ	pear
ナス	eggplant
にんじん	carrot

パイナップル	pineapple	とり肉	chicken
バナナ	banana	ドーナツ	donut
パパイヤ	papaya	肉	meat
ブロッコリー	broccoli	ハム	ham
ぶどう	grapes	ハンバーガー	hamburger
ほうれん草	spinach	パスタ	pasta
マッシュルーム	mushroom	パン	bread
マンゴ	mango	ピザ	pizza
みかん	mandarin orange	ファーストフード	fast food
メロン	melon	豚肉	pork
桃	peach	フライドチキン	fried chicken
りんご	apple	フライドポテト	French fries
レタス	lettuce	プリン	pudding
		ベーコン	bacon

(2) 食品・食材 (Food Items, Foodstuffs)

アイスクリーム	ice cream	ホットケーキ	pancake
イカ	squid	ホットドッグ	hot dog
うなぎ	eel	味噌汁	miso soup
エビ	shrimp, lobster	麺類	noodles
おにぎり	rice ball	緑茶、日本茶	green tea
オムレツ	omelet		

5 外食 (Eating Out)
(1) 様々な場所 (Types of Place)

貝	shellfish	カフェ	cafe
牡蠣	oyster	喫茶店	coffee shop
カニ	crab	バー	bar
カレーライス	curry and rice	レストラン、食堂	restaurant / fast-food
牛肉	beef		restaurant / family restaurant
牛乳	milk		

(2) 国別料理 (Types of Food by Country)

魚介類	seafood	アメリカ料理	American
クッキー	cookie	イタ飯	Italian
ケーキ	cake	韓国料理	Korean
コーヒー	coffee	西洋料理	Western
紅茶	tea	タイ料理	Thai
ご飯	rice	中華料理	Chinese
魚	fish	フランス料理	French
サラダ	salad	無国籍料理	international cuisine
サンドイッチ	sandwich	メキシコ料理	Mexican
シュークリーム	cream puff	和食	Japanese
シリアル	cereal		

(3) その他 (Other)

スープ	soup	営業時間	opening hours
寿司	sushi	(〜 曜日に)開店	(be) open on 〜
ステーキ	steak	カウンター	counter
スパゲティー	spaghetti	飾り付け	decoration
ソーセージ	sausage	勘定書	check / bill
タコ	octopus		
漬物	pickles		
トースト	toast		

勘定書をもらう	get / ask for the check / bill
最初の料理	starter
スタイル	style
（食事の）席	table
チェーン店	chain（restaurant）
昼食	lunch
注文	order
朝食	breakfast
付け合せ	side dish
定食	set meal
店内で食べる	eat in
飲み物	drink
民営	private business
メインの料理	main course
メニュー	menu
持ち帰る	take away
（〜 曜日に）閉店	（be）closed on 〜
夕食	dinner

6 よく使う形容詞（Useful Adjectives）

明るい	bright
居心地のよい	cozy
田舎の	rural
印象的な	impressive
丘の多い	hilly
面白い	interesting
活気のある	lively
閑静な、静かな	quiet
簡単な、楽な	easy
奇抜な	original
くつろげる	relaxing
暗い	dark
景色のよい	scenic
郊外の	suburban
混み合った	crowded
騒がしい	noisy
山地の	mountainous
親しみやすい	friendly
少量の	small
退屈な	boring
高い	expensive
楽しい	fun
疲れる	tiring

都会の	urban
にぎやかな	busy
不便な	inconvenient
便利な	convenient
難しい、面倒な	difficult
役に立つ	useful
安い	cheap
リーゾナブルな	reasonable
量が多い	big

7 犯罪関連語句 （Words to Describe Crimes）
（1）外見 （Appearance）

中背の	average height
普通の体格の	average build / medium weight
太りぎみの	heavy-set / overweight / fat
やせ型の	thin / slightly built / slim
髭（ひげ）	beard
三十代の	in one's thirties
中年の	middle-aged

（2）服装／持ち物 （Clothing, Belongings）

毛糸の帽子	woolly hat, woolen hat
拳銃	gun, pistol, revolver
コート	coat
サングラス	sunglasses
スカーフ	scarf
スニーカー	sneakers
ズボン	pants, trousers
ブーツ	boots
覆面、マスク	mask
ヘッドスカーフ	headscarf
メガネ	glasses

（3）その他 （Other）

銀行員	bank clerk
銀行の窓口係	teller
強盗(行為)	robbery
強盗(人)	robber
〜に銃を向ける	point a gun at 〜
盗む	rob

著　者

Julyan Nutt（ジュリアン・ナット）　東海学園大学

Michael Marshall（マイケル・マーシャル）　東海学園大学

倉橋洋子（くらはし　ようこ）　東海学園大学名誉教授

宮田学（みやた　まなぶ）　名古屋市立大学名誉教授

コミュニケーションのための実践英語 3 [準中級編]

2020 年 3 月 30 日　第 1 版発行
2024 年 2 月 20 日　第 4 版発行

著　　者──Julyan Nutt / Michael Marshall / 倉橋洋子 /
　　　　　宮田学

発 行 者──前田俊秀

発 行 所──株式会社 三修社
　　　　　〒150-0001東京都渋谷区神宮前2-2-22
　　　　　TEL 03-3405-4511　FAX 03-3405-4522
　　　　　振替 00190-9-72758
　　　　　https://www.sanshusha.co.jp
　　　　　編集担当 三井るり子

印 刷 所──港北メディアサービス株式会社

©2020 Printed in Japan ISBN978-4-384-33499-9 C1082

表紙デザイン──峯岸孝之
本文デザイン・DTP──株式会社 明昌堂
本文イラスト──藤原ヒロコ
準拠音声録音──ELEC（吹込み：Neil DeMaere / Rachel Walzer）
準拠音声制作──高速録音株式会社

教科書準拠CD発売

本書の準拠CDをご希望の方は弊社までお問い合わせください。